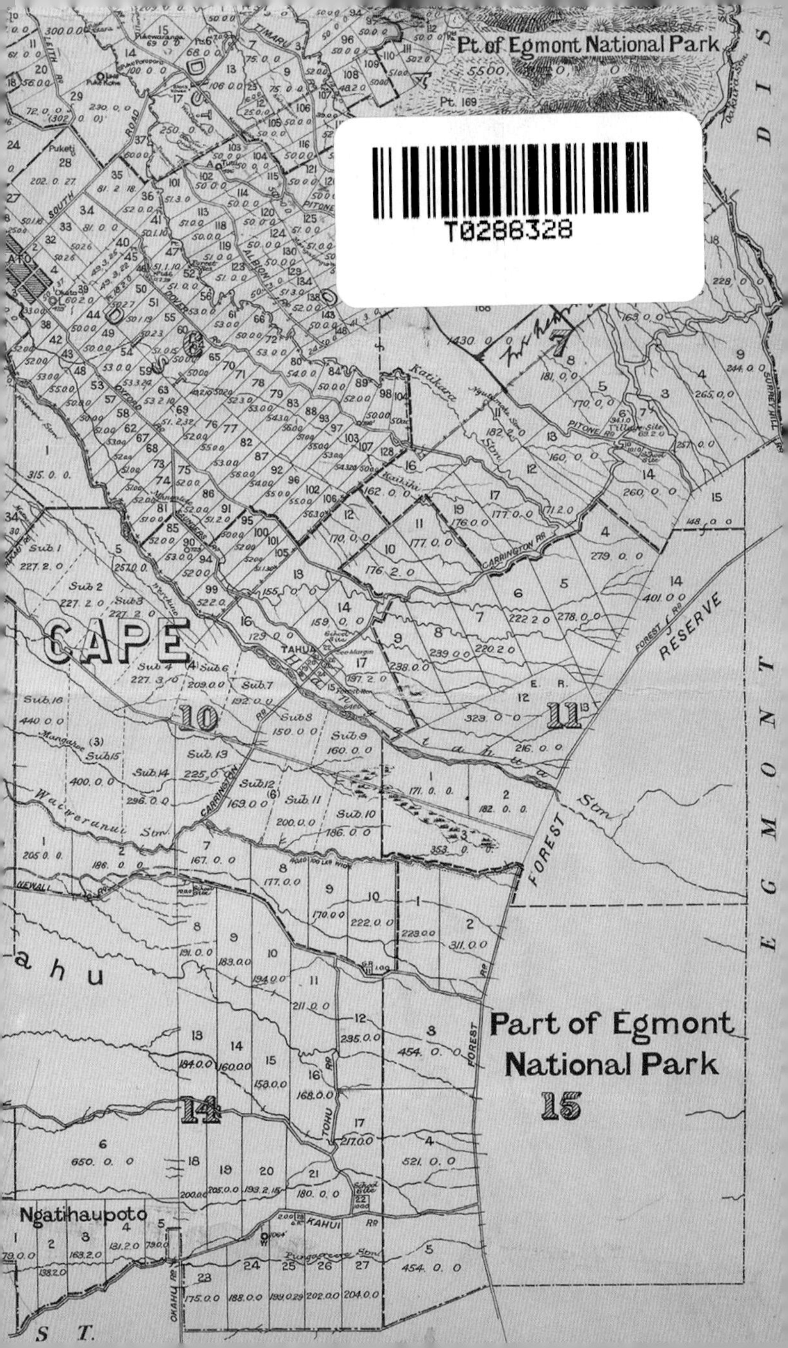

Pt. of Egmont National Park
5500
TIMARU
SOUTH ROAD
ALBION
DOVER
OXFORD
PITONE RD
SURREY HILL RD
Katikara
CARRINGTON RD
CAPE
10
11
TAHUA
RESERVE
FOREST RD
E. R.
Waiweranui Stm
CARRINGTON
NEWALL
FOREST
EGMONT
DIS
Part of Egmont
National Park
15
14
TOHU RD
KAHUI RD
OKAHU RD
Ngatihaupoto
S T.

Block IV
Waiweranui Stm.
Dairy Factory
Pt.1
RIGHT OF WAY
SOUTH RD
Pikitahi
Scale
Chs.
Teikuparua
STENT ROAD
WAREA
Warea
Tarakihi
NEWALL
Mangahume Stm.
COAST RD
Ihutangi
SOUTH
Te Pua
Okawa
Waitekauri
Tuku
Kapoaiaia
PUNGAREHU ROAD
Cape Egmont
Wairere
Waiohau
LIGHT HOUSE
Drain Res.
CAPE ROAD
PUNGAREHU
Otahi
PARIHAKA ROAD
PARAPARA
Mataurukuhia
Puhina
Tipoka
Waitotoroa
TIPOKA ROAD
Te Araiotawhiki
Otuakaje
Wairua
Pehu
Mangaroa
OPOURAPA

The Forgotten Coast

The Forgotten Coast

Richard Shaw

MASSEY UNIVERSITY PRESS

This book is for Camille and Rosalie,
for whom the forgetting can end, and for
Ema, who never forgot in the first place.

The lie of the sign, if I can put it
that way, is in what it doesn't say,
in the facts it leaves out.

— Rachel Buchanan,
The Parihaka Album: Lest We Forget

Contents

Prologue

There are many possible beginnings to this book. I have chosen to start with an ending. It is Christmas Eve 2012 and my father is dying, unable to find his way back to us after heart surgery that had been described as routine but which quickly became complicated. There is a moment when we think we have him back; when it looks for all money as if he is about to make it to the surface. But his arms flail, his eyes do not regain focus and he sinks away into the depths.

He dies as he lived — quietly, with little fuss, not wishing to bother anyone. There are grace notes. The young priest who wears cherry-red Docs; the gentle phone call at 3 a.m. suggesting we make our way to Dad's bedside; my mother, whose tenderness and composure as her man leaves her I find breathtaking. I kiss his forehead and set out for the toilet with my sister Bridget, only to be called back. By the time we are with him again he has gone. Quietly. Without fuss. You'd almost not know. It is ten years since he died, and I often find myself back in that hospital room looking down at his broad forehead.

Ursula Le Guin talks about digging answers out, down there in the deep regions of the self.[1] Not an easy nor ever a brief process, but one which my father's death starts in me. You have to be wary of singling out particular events and saying: '*This* is when it began,' for doing that can give things a false sense of tidiness. But it can also prevent life from endlessly flowing through your fingers, and that is one of many things Dad's dying did. It dragged to the surface a process of reflection and introspection that may have begun long before but which by then was pointlessly meandering along. It began to come into focus in Hamilton Hospital on Christmas Eve 2012. Fathers, sons — and further back, behind those things, land, belief and belonging. That's what this book is about.

One last thing before leaping in. In the Tom Stoppard play *Arcadia*, Hannah says: 'It's wanting to know that makes us matter. Otherwise we're going out the way we came in.'[2] This is a personal account — I own it. From time to time I refer to my family. When I do so I invariably have in mind either my own family (Ema, Camille and Rosalie) or my family of origin (Mum, Dad and my sisters, Barbara, Bridget and Jane) rather than the wider network of aunties, uncles and cousins on Mum's and Dad's sides. I wouldn't presume to know, far less to speak for, their views on issues that, for me, remain troubling and unresolved. It is not my place to do that. It is, on the other hand, my place to make sense of matters that reach far back into my past — for I've no wish to go out the way I came in.

Start here

In a corner of a forgotten room in the Pontifical Lateran University in Rome lies a thesis on the intrinsic evil of the lie. It was written in 1932 by Richard Thomas Gilhooly, my great-uncle and a twenty-one-year-old student of the Pontifical Irish College. The work was submitted for a doctorate of divinity, the exam for which was exhaustive, stretching over two weeks and covering papers on dogma, speculative moral philosophy and church tract, as well as a public defence of the thesis. It was also exhausting, so exacting that at some point during his preparation for the ordeal Richard contracted the tuberculosis that was to blight his life and kill him before he turned fifty.

The bare bones of the story are that Dick — as he was called by everyone other than the Latins, to whom he was Ricardus — was twenty years old when he arrived in Rome from the Holy Cross Seminary in Mosgiel, twenty-one when he completed his doctorate, twenty-two when he was ordained a priest and forty-four when he died. But bare bones are never enough. Dick completed three degrees during the twenty-two months he spent living on the Via dei Ss Quattro, just 400 metres from the Colosseum. At the time the doctorate of divinity was a four-year programme (and about to be bumped up to five), but he knocked it off in two.

Because he was two years shy of the official age for ordination he had to obtain a papal dispensation from Pius XI in order to celebrate his first Mass at the old Catholic cathedral on Buckle Street in Wellington. (The minimum age for ordination at the time was twenty-four years, although with the pope's blessing that could be reduced by eighteen months: Dick had to wait a year until he could even qualify for the dispensation.) He had been singled out by the Catholic hierarchy for post-doctoral study in the United States and England, but spent the second half of his life in and out of hospitals and catering to the parishioners of Carterton, Takapau, Masterton and Tākaka.

He has fascinated me for years, this priest-uncle of mine, and not only because of the appeal of a narrative arc that stretches from Pungarehu, the small coastal Taranaki town where Dick grew up and of which not much now remains, to the Eternal City and back again. Neither does the attraction entirely lie in the tragedy of a brilliant career wrecked by disease (although on this point Dick and I disagree: his later letters indicate he was quite content to come home to work in a local parish). Beyond the obvious there is something that happens when I use Dick as a lens through which to peer into my past. He refracts time, both forwards and backwards, in disturbing and compelling ways.

So do two other men, one who has always been with me one way or another and the second a much more recent arrival. The latecomer is Dick's father, Andrew Gilhooly, who was part of the armed force that invaded Parihaka in early November 1881 and who was, later, a farmer on the 'great knuckle' of land that had been confiscated from Māori — 'rebel' and loyalist alike — in 1865.[1] As bare bones go I find these ones deeply disturbing. They concern events that are at the heart of this country's understanding of itself but which remain bitterly contested, in interpretation if not in fact.

We may be a farming nation (even if most of us have nothing much to do with the land any more), but in Taranaki the ground on which that farming takes place was taken from the people to whom it belonged. So in recent years Andrew has come to intrigue me, too; but whereas I approach Dick with a clean, clear sense of anticipation, Andrew is someone I have to come to terms with. With him the need to understand is a compulsion rather than a pleasure, one that comes from his role in one of the defining episodes in the violent enforcement of colonial rule in Aotearoa, and from the significance that involvement holds for me today.

The third man, Bob, is my father. His real name was Keith, but I never heard anyone call him that. His family had a way with names: Keith was Bob, Dianne was Mickey, Betty was Tim. When we were kids Dad would say 'K is for Bob', which made no sense whatsoever. He was a gentle, thoughtful man who spent the early years of his life in and out of hospitals and in a Masterton orphanage, and most of the rest of it dedicated to the family he had with Mum. Although he was in Wellington for only a couple of years while training to become a teacher, he was a 'townie' to my mother's people on the Coast.

He knew nothing about cars or carpentry and didn't have much of a shed, but he was good in a kitchen and could wash dishes with his bare hands in scalding water. His sense of humour was on the dry side of flinty: the first time he and Mum went to the cinema he bought her a box of Queen Anne chocolates but said he'd found it under the seat. She believed him.

He had a big and compassionate heart (although not a well one, as we would learn) and much preferred working with the hardcase kids from the forgotten parts of New Plymouth than the ones from the leafy suburbs of Vogeltown and Brooklands. He was good at that work, and when he died some of those kids, grown now, filed in and sat quietly at the back of St Joseph's Church in New Plymouth, slipping away as we carried him out. Especially in his later years, when his heart began to give up the ghost, Dad was a little like Owen Marshall's old man Trumpeter, 'watching one word out of sight before releasing the next'.[2]

Dad spoke a particular kind of emotional language, one born of the years spent growing up in an institution at a time when men used words to express themselves sparingly if at all. It was a language built on silence as much as on words. For many years I misunderstood those silences. It has taken his death for me to realise that his was an eloquent tongue of love and affection — one I never really learned to speak with him.

I have always been surrounded by formidable women. I live in a family of women, my partner and our two daughters. All three are smarter than I am, and less naïve. I have three sisters and a mother, all highly competent in their chosen fields. I have, or have had, aunts, great-aunts, and grandmothers (neither of whom I met). And one of my great-grandmothers is pivotal to this story. Still, this book is largely about men, a choice that may sit poorly with some. But it is the men in my life I need to have words with at the moment, not the women.[3]

I don't pretend that this is a family history, much less one that is genealogically researched to within an inch of its life. For one thing, I don't have many of the foundational dates or events that often characterise the histories of settler families. The names of ships, dates of arrival and so forth are largely missing, and those that do slip in are unreliable from time to time. For another, especially in the early pages, I have no interest in telling a conventional settler narrative, one that speaks of thrusting progress and economic productivity but which dances lightly over the confiscation, theft and violence that made possible the good stuff. I am much more concerned with figuring out the *un*settling effect that the arrival of my ancestors on the Coast had on the people who were already there.[4]

So, less a family history than an attempt to address a couple of questions that Rachel Buchanan poses at the end of her book *The Parihaka Album: Lest We Forget*. Buchanan's impact on me owes much to her knack for using words in ways that bring me up short, and to the questions — explicit and tacit — she poses. On the last page are two final queries: What stories do your dead tell you? How do you see your past? I'd been struggling to explain to myself what this book was about, and having difficulty finding a way of fitting these three men into a single account. Buchanan solved the conundrum for me.

This book is about one man I love, a second I am fascinated by and a third who is at the heart of it all. It is a response to Buchanan's challenges. What I didn't immediately see was the relationship between the two questions: how answering the first would profoundly change my understanding of the second.

There is a small personal connection here, too. In the late 1970s Rachel played Dorothy in a New Plymouth Operatic Society production of *The Wizard of Oz*. My old and dear friend Bernard Leuthart played the Scarecrow and I was the Tin Man.[5] Rachel was younger, and I don't recall spending much time with her. Lately, though, I have read everything she has written on Parihaka that I can lay my hands on. Her work is important, razor-sharp and beautifully written, and it crops up repeatedly in these pages.

It is not as if I am sending stories of these three men out into the void, because of course there have long been family tales that frame each of them. Andrew the armed constable-turned-farmer, Dick the scholarly prodigy, Bob the orphan who had a family. But — and this is especially so with Andrew — these accounts are muted and often incomplete. Details are left out, forgotten or unaccounted for. This book is my attempt to fill in some of the silences that surround these men, and in doing so to better understand things that I am still trying to figure out for myself. Fathers, sons, land and lies. My own past, present and possible futures.

None of this is straightforward and much of it is fraught, because it entails interfering with family stories. These kinds of stories matter, for it is through their telling and retelling that we remember ourselves and 'keep alive those who only live now in the telling'.[6] That is the purpose of families' narratives: to give shape and coherence to things, and to launch memories of the past out into the future. They are both *of* a family and also *outside* of it.

But family stories can also be dangerous — far from anodyne and never neutral. They are a sort of public property: some are more or less sacrosanct, while others are battle sites, fiercely contested. These you tangle with at your peril.

I think it was W. H. Auden who talked of the 'biddable dead'; of the way in which we recruit particular memories of those who are gone and put them to work to ensure that things are remembered *just so*. Sometimes that means not telling certain stories, or altering them so they are fit for wider consumption. Or remaining silent, hushed, as if this will help us 'deftly steer our way around the past'.[7]

We approach such accounts with caution and care, and often with trepidation. The more so when our own stories intrude on those of other people. Most of all, perhaps, when a thing long forgotten is uncovered in the telling.

5 November 1881

Shortly before 7 a.m. on 5 November 1881 my great-grandfather, Andrew Gilhooly, stood alongside 1588 other men waiting to begin te pāhua (the plunder) of Parihaka. As a member of the Armed Constabulary's (AC) No. 3 Company, which remained garrisoned at Parihaka until well into 1885, it is probable that he also took part in the subsequent destruction of the pā and its cultivations during the weeks and months that followed the invasion.

In this country you can no longer simply put statements like these quietly aside (although that is exactly what I have done for the better part of fifty years). They must be comprehended and made sense of. Above all else, for me, they need coming to terms with.

There are two parts to this. The first requires uncovering something of who my great-grandfather was, and how he came to be both in this country and a member of the AC. I have never known much about either. I am not an historian so I was unaware of the distinction between a person's past and their history until Rachel Buchanan introduced me to it. The first includes all those things we have our own personal memories of, while the second captures the wider sweep of events we find ourselves caught up in. Andrew doesn't feature in my past. There are enough stories about his wife and kids to fill a paddock but I don't really know any about him. He's increasingly a part of my history, though, so I need to get to know him.

The second requirement is to set out why the AC were ranged outside the pā in the early hours of 5 November 1881. That matters because what came after Parihaka — for Andrew and for his wife Kate, for his son Dick, and certainly for me — makes a pale sort of sense until it is put alongside what came before. The 'very big stories' (the colonisation of Aotearoa) and the 'very little stories' (my great-grandfather's part in that process) are always intertwined,[1] and the step from high politics to the lives and times of individuals is not so terribly big. So I need to touch on the large historical truth in which the small personal truth about my great-grandfather sits.[2] In short, I need to both discover Andrew and bear witness to what happened under the mountain.

Andrew was an Irishman, and on Mum's father's side my family's time in this country begins with him. He was born in 1855, six years after the end of the Great Famine. One of ten children, Andrew was the son of tenant farming people who paid £26 10s a year to William Anderson Esq. for the privilege of working two small pieces of land — one of 27 acres and the other only 2 acres (and separated by about half a kilometre) — in Ballynagreanagh, a small townland in Kilteely Parish, in the east of County Limerick and on the border with County Tipperary.[3]

He came to this country in 1874. I know he was still in Ireland in 1873 because there is an Irish court record indicating that on 5 July that year he was sentenced to a month in prison with hard labour, having been convicted of assault and rescue.[4] There are no details about the assault (or the rescue), but intriguingly his older brother John and his father, Hugh, were also tied up in the shenanigans. The three of them appeared together in the Limerick Magistrates Court on the same charge, pleaded guilty and were convicted and sentenced to '1 Cal Mnth with H. L.'.

That same day, one James O'Donnell was sentenced to three months in prison for receiving tuppence under false pretences. A Michael Roche pleaded guilty to stealing a penknife and appears to have been given three choices of punishment: pay a fine of £1 and costs of £1 6s, accept a fortnight's prison or submit to a dozen strokes of the lash. Wisely, he went with option one.

'Growing up in Ireland meant preparing yourself to leave it,'[5] and perhaps this brush with the law was all the encouragement Andrew needed to clear out to the other side of world, because five months after his brief spell inside he took assisted passage as a single man on board the New Zealand Shipping Company's 882-ton clipper *Wennington*. The hard labour had the same effect on John, although he decamped to the United States.[6]

The *Wennington* sailed from Gravesend, on the Thames in Kent, on 21 January 1874 and arrived in Wellington on 25 May. Among the 294 passengers aboard were eighty Kentish villagers who thought they were heading for the province of Canterbury; indeed, some of them had originally applied to go to South Australia. Instead, they all wound up in Wellington.

The 124-day journey, during which three children died and ten were born, was an especially long one (on average the trip took around a hundred days). The ship had been so long overdue that, as the *New Zealand Mail* reported, among those waiting for her the impression 'was generally felt, though not expressed, that some serious misfortune had misfallen her'. It was eventually decided that an exceptionally large cargo of iron explained its protracted journey. In any event, the commissioners who inspected the ship 'found the immigrants to be a healthy lot of people, free from organic disease of any kind . . . all seemed well pleased with the voyage, and expressed themselves as quite satisfied with the treatment they had received'.[7]

Andrew Gilhooly is described in the ship's record as a farm labourer from Limerick, the portrayal that follows him through his military history. But he is also said to be twenty-one years of age, which makes him three years older than he should have been. Such anomalies aside, it seems certain that Andrew arrived here in mid-1874.

That appears even more plausible when I come across

a note written many years later by Andrew's youngest daughter, my Great-aunt Liz, in which she indicates that her father arrived in New Zealand with his sister Bridget. There is, indeed, a Bridget on the *Wennington* when it docks in Wellington — only her name is spelt Gluley. Bridget Gluley, a twenty-three-year-old dairymaid from Limerick. Say 'Gilhooly' and 'Gluley' out loud and they sound identical, so I suspect that this is a phonetic spelling, as might happen when a harried young shipping or immigration clerk takes a stab at spelling the unusual Irish name.

'Gilhooly' may not be the most elegant of names, but it comes from far back in the Irish past. It is an anglicisation of the Gaelic name Mac Giolla Ghuala ('son of the servant of Ghuala'), a subclan of the O'Mulveys. The homelands of the Mac Giolla Ghuala were the counties of Roscommon and Leitrim (there are records of three Gilhooly men who served as priests in Country Leitrim between 1461 and 1505), but Andrew's branch of the Gilhooly sept moved to Ballynagreanagh in Limerick in the eighteenth century. So the name may be a bit of a mouthful, but it has pedigree.[8]

The *Wennington*'s records show that Andrew got off in Wellington while Bridget travelled on to Westland, perhaps in order to be among other Irish, many of whom congregated in mining districts.[9] She is still there twenty years later. In 1892 thc parliamcntary rccord includes a document called 'Immigrants' Unpaid Promissory

Notes', which shows 'the number and amounts of unpaid promissory notes given by assisted immigrants now in the different Immigration Offices throughout the colony for passages from the Home-country'.[10] In Hokitika, B. Gluley still owes £1.

For years I blithely assumed that the Irish migrated in large numbers to Aotearoa. At school I was surrounded by them (Mum once estimated that fifty-two cousins of various familial denominations were with me at Francis Douglas), which may explain this misapprehension. In fact, the Irish made up only 20 per cent or so of those who migrated here from the United Kingdom between 1800 and 1945.[11] At its peak, in 1886, the Irish-born population of the colony numbered a little over 51,000 — around half of whom were Catholic — which comprised roughly 10 per cent of the overall population of half a million.[12]

To some extent this reflected anti-Irish — and especially anti-Irish Catholic — attitudes. For a sizeable portion of the population '"Ireland" represented not an oppressed homeland or a glorious cause but unrest, violence, disloyalty and the dangers of Roman Catholicism'.[13] Such attitudes were sufficiently entrenched to lead Keith Sinclair to conclude that New Zealand 'was the only British colony where it was both possible and conceptually necessary to completely purge the Irish from national and historical consciousness'.[14]

In the early waves of migration the New Zealand Company much preferred its migrants to come from

Protestant Ulster, while in the 1870s anti-Catholic discrimination in the allocation of assisted places by the government's agent-general in London, Isaac Featherston, triggered protests from aspiring Irish migrants. Featherston had form on this. In 1857, as the first superintendent of the Wellington province (he had also been the MP for Whanganui in the very first colonial parliament, represented Wellington for six parliamentary terms and served as a minister in the Fox governments), he had specifically asked the province's UK recruiting agents not to grant assisted passage to Irish Catholics. He was still at it twenty years later, politely explaining to the minister for immigration 'that I have always regarded the emigrants drawn from the North of Ireland as of a very desirable character'.[15] The inference is that people like Andrew and Bridget Gilhooly were not.

The broader politics of immigration at the time were also fraught. Speaking in the parliament in June 1870, Colonial Treasurer Julius Vogel thundered that '[w]e do not hesitate to declare that if, as has been proposed, the Imperial Government enter upon the task of directly exporting a portion of the idle masses, the Colonial Parliaments will have to jealously watch the class of persons sent out, and, if needs be, by legislation to prevent the Colonies from being converted into receptacles for the worst form of refuse population'.[16] There is no suggestion that Vogel had Irish Catholics in mind when he spoke, but plenty — Featherston and his ilk — would have.

I can't make up my mind on Vogel's position regarding the Irish. On the one hand, in the same month that Andrew Gilhooly arrived in Aotearoa — May 1874 — Vogel took it upon himself 'to impress upon [Featherston] that the character of the class of immigrants now arriving is a source of very grave anxiety to the Government, and is creating great uneasiness in the colony. I have already been officially informed that the shipment by the *Asia* to Dunedin includes a number of girls out of the Cork workhouse, some of whom are notoriously loose.'[17]

Barely a month later, however, he writes to Featherston again, offering '[a]nother suggestion which I desire you will give effect to, [which is] that a certain quantity of salt fish be in future shipped for the use of Roman Catholic emigrants, who, from the non-issue of this article of diet upon their fast days, are either deprived altogether of their dinners, or are driven, against their feelings, to transgress the rules of their Church'.[18]

So much for the small story of how Andrew Gilhooly came to be in this country. Now to an account of something altogether more consequential. Parihaka had been established in 1866 by Te Whiti o Rongomai and Tohu Kākahi, both of whom were of Taranaki and Te Ātiawa iwi.[19] The pā became 'a haven for all dispossessed and a shrine for all hapū', attracting those 'amassed from the north, south and east, scattered by confiscation'.[20] At the time of its desecration, Parihaka — named either for the 'lamentations of earlier occupants' or for its location between hills[21] — had a population of around 1500 and was said to be the most prosperous Māori settlement in the country.

It had a bank and bakery, was surrounded by extensive cultivations on which were deployed state-of-the-art reaping and threshing machines, and was organisationally capable of providing hospitality for the thousands who attended its monthly meetings.[22] The pā made perfect sense in the context of the New Zealand Constitution Act 1852, which set up the early New Zealand state and which clearly anticipated the establishment of territory in which Māori authority would prevail.

In mid-1878, however, the colonial government began surveying and settling Taranaki land that it had confiscated in 1865 under the provisions of the New Zealand Settlement Act 1863. Although the policy was ostensibly aimed at 'rebellious' iwi in Taranaki, the Waikato and the Bay of Plenty — that is, at people who had resisted the Crown's attempts to take their land — in practice, Māori who had not taken up arms against the Crown (including the people of Parihaka) or who had been its allies also lost their land.

In Taranaki, the administration of confiscated land descended into a 'mire of confusion', and by the mid-1870s most of the land had been effectively abandoned by the government.[23]

Not by its original inhabitants, however, many of whom

had moved back onto the land once it seemed clear that the government had walked away from it. (Ministers chose to see this differently, complaining of the difficulties they had had 'preventing the Natives from creeping back upon land which the Government were not at the time able to occupy'.)[24]

The surveys were seen as 'the sharp end of the otherwise blunt confiscation process'.[25] The first ones took place on Ngāti Ruanui land on the Waimate Plains in south Taranaki. Te Whiti, whose mana extended the full length of the west coast, ordered that the surveyors be removed from the plains, and so 'quietly, thoroughly, and good humouredly [Māori] packed up each survey camp, loaded horses and drays, and carted everything back across the Waingongoro'.[26]

The following year the government sought to lay the political groundwork for the survey and sale of the entire Taranaki area. In a 'symbolic assertion of proprietorship',[27] on 25 May 1879 Te Whiti and Tohu sent men to plough land on the Pitone Road near Oakura, where the Second Taranaki War — an attritional conflict that had less to do with disputed land purchases (as was the case with the first war at Waitara) than with land confiscation[28] — had begun.

In keeping with their pacifist teachings, the ploughers were unarmed, and over the coming weeks they also ploughed settler-occupied land at seven locations from Pukearuhe in the north to Hāwera in the south. The symbolism is pretty hard to miss: 'The sword had been replaced by the biblical representation of peace, the ploughshare, but the ploughshare was being used to plough lands unjustly obtained.'[29]

Te Whiti and Tohu's strategy — which was decided upon only after other alternatives had been considered[30] — is usually described as passive resistance. In fact, it was extremely active.[31] What is more, the tactics extended well beyond non-violent protest to incorporate a range of forms of non-violent intervention, persuasion, and social and political non-cooperation.[32]

In keeping with its own decidedly non-pacifist methods, the government retaliated by making widespread arrests. Some 420 ploughers were eventually imprisoned, forty of whom were brought to trial in New Plymouth, where they were found guilty of 'malicious injury to property'.[33] The remainder were incarcerated, initially in Wellington and subsequently in Hokitika and Dunedin, and on Rīpapa Island in Lyttelton Harbour. The inconvenience of having a sizeable group of men imprisoned for actions that broke no law was initially taken care of by the Confiscated Land Inquiry and Maori Prisoners' Trials Act 1879, which retrospectively validated the arrests of the ploughers and gave the governor the right to hold them without charge and to defer their trials. The Maori Prisoners' Act 1880 legalised the prisoners' detention and dispensed with the need for trials entirely.

There was some parliamentary opposition to these measures. During the debate on the 1879 legislation, for instance, one member argued vehemently that 'by passing this measure the House would be indorsing [*sic*] a species of legislation of a very dangerous and unprecedented character'.[34] The response to that concern by the native minister, John Bryce, tells you all you need to know about the administration's commitment to constitutional niceties. To him, both Magna Carta and the principle of *habeas corpus* (the ancient legal principle that protects citizens against unlawful and indefinite detention by the state) were 'mere legal technicalities', and he could entirely see 'that the circumstances of the country might occasionally demand that [*habeas corpus*] should be set aside'.[35]

In mid-1880 the AC, my great-grandfather included, was pushing through a military road linking Ōkato and Ōpunake. The South Road would also facilitate military access to Parihaka — something Te Whiti had long foreseen — prompting Buchanan to describe its construction as the 'first attack' on Parihaka.[36] In the process, armed constables routinely destroyed fences that kept livestock out of Parihaka's extensive cultivations. 'Fencing out hostility',[37] Tohu and Te Whiti's fencers put them back up. Sometimes, too, a 'party composed of over a hundred very small children (in the charge of an adult) designated the tatarakihi (locusts) were sent out from Parihaka to traverse the road through the cultivation, warbling, like a flock of blight birds, an incantation taught them by Tohu'.[38]

In July 1880 the summary arrests began again. Two hundred and sixteen fencers would eventually be shipped to prisons in the South Island.[39] In the Maori Prisoners Detention Act, which took effect on 6 August 1880, Te Whiti's fencers received their very own piece of legislation denying them the right to a trial.

The day before that legislation came into force, the West Coast Commission, established in early 1880, concluded that 'broken promises, unfulfilled Compensation Court decisions, and fraud had justified Maori protests'.[40] But without having talked with Māori leadership (the Commission declined invitations to visit Parihaka), it also took upon itself the right to decide that Māori would agree with the government's intention to keep (and sell) confiscated land as long as native reserves were provided for.

On that basis it recommended stopping the surveying and sale of land until such reserves had been set aside, pointing out that 'filling our gaols with prisoners, not for crimes but for political offences in which there is no sign of criminal intent', had done nothing to advance the peace.[41] Under pressure, the government began releasing the prisoners held in the South Island in batches.

Extraordinarily, however, the native minister also announced his intention to *re*commence the survey and sale of the coastal portion of the Parihaka Block. Bryce had fought in the Taranaki wars and had once described Te Whiti as 'far gone in insanity' during a parliamentary debate.[42] (On another occasion he made reference to 'the supernatural *mana* of Te Whiti'. Bryce was clearly unsettled by the Parihaka leader.)[43] His predecessor as native minister, John Sheehan, had proposed to the West Coast Commission that the entire Parihaka Block, from the mountain to the sea, should comprise a native reserve (on condition of the owners' good behaviour).

But Bryce, with his eyes on the fertile coastal parts of Parihaka and wary of the political threat posed by Tohu and Te Whiti, took a much less forgiving view. He also had a strong desire to invade Parihaka that he did not bother to conceal. Bryce was briefly replaced as native minister by a somewhat less belligerent William Rolleston, but duly reinstated when his successor proved to be insufficiently belligerent.

And at this point another of my ancestors makes an entrance. In October 1881 Michael Fleming, one of my great-grandmother's half-brothers, buys Section 22 Block 12 of the Cape Survey District. Michael had emigrated in 1875, and the section is the first of sixteen in Block 12 that he and his brothers, Richard and James, will eventually own.[44] Later that month Michael's attempts at fencing are disrupted by local Māori. Lieutenant Colonel Roberts, the AC's commanding officer in Taranaki, picks up the story:

> During [October 1881] about fifty Maoris assembled on land belonging to Mr. Fleming, a settler near Cape Egmont lighthouse, while he was fencing on his land, and told him

> to leave off, at the same time carrying away the fencing material with the exception of some heavy posts, which they cut in two. On a subsequent occasion Mr. Fleming was molested, and before a force could be got on the ground the Natives had retired. The district by this time was in a very unsettled state.[45]

The encounter was also cited, at greater length, in a telegram Roberts sent to Premier John Hall on 19 October, which Hall referred to in his own correspondence with Governor Arthur Gordon on 24 October in which he set out the case for the invasion.[46] The Roberts telegram reads:

> Have just returned from Section 28. Fleming and his mate were working in the bush on Section 22 this morning, cutting and carrying out posts, when about fifty Maoris came to them and told them to leave off work, at the same time carrying back the posts which Fleming had carried to the road-side. At first they spoke only in Maori, but subsequently told them in English to stop. Besides this, over two hundred small posts for a sod-and-wire fence, which were laid along the road frontage of 28, have been carried off the land, and thrown into the flax and fern, and some into a swamp . . . Fleming told us that his brother, and joint owner of the two sections mentioned, was in New Plymouth, and expected out soon with the wire for the fence. I recommended him not to take the wire on to the land at present, and not to go on with the fence again until I had received your instructions on the matter . . .

> Maoris are working today in a small unfenced clearing in Section 43, Block XII, near the road. This clearing was pointed out to you from the whares on Section 44.

A little over a decade later Andrew Gilhooly will gain legal title to Section 44, but in 1881, just a month before he is part of the military action against Parihaka, there are still Māori whare on that land. Here are the first signs of the tides of colonial history swirling around my ancestors.

With tensions fuelled by bellicose media speculation on the warlike intentions of the recently returned former prisoners, and with the imminent return from Fiji of Governor Gordon (who was felt to be overly sympathetic to Māori), at 4 a.m. on 20 October 1881 Bryce spirited a government proclamation out of Wellington and hastened north by road. Two days later Bryce's secretary, W. J. Butler, read the proclamation out at Parihaka, exhorting people to leave the pā and accept the reserve land the government fully intended to offer them or suffer 'the great evil which must fall on them'.[47]

The 'great evil' arrived early on the morning of 5 November when 644 AC and 945 Volunteer troops, led by John Bryce on his white charger, marched on Parihaka. The better to conceal subsequent abuses, media coverage of what then occurred was suppressed — although not altogether successfully, as a couple of special correspondents made their way through the bush around to the rear of the pā where they were given a whare from which they could watch the day's proceedings.

All the same, it would be two years before any official record of that day would appear in Aotearoa.[48] That it did so at all is only because in 1882 the parliamentary opposition in London successfully forced the tabling of a 'Correspondence respecting Native Affairs in New Zealand and the Imprisonment of Certain Maoris' in the House of Commons.[49] The document was subsequently published in British parliamentary papers. As a result, it became known that:

> Parihaka had been taken without resistance; that it was 'completely broken up'; that about 1500 men, women, and children had been arrested; and that six were imprisoned, including Te Whiti and Tohu, who were held on charges of sedition. Titokowaru, who had recently returned from prison with the ploughmen, was imprisoned again for failing to procure sureties to keep the peace. Images of a fuller picture escaped later to the public arena; images of assaults; rape; looting; pillage; theft; the destruction of homes and of hundreds of hectares of crops; the forced relocation of 1556 persons without money, food, or shelter; the introduction of passes for Maori to facilitate the military's control of movements in the area; and the suspension of trials and other legal safeguards when it appeared that lawful convictions might not be achieved.[50]

Te pāhua o Parihaka — where 'the Crown responded to peace with tyranny, to unity with division, and to autonomy with oppression'[51] — has come to exemplify the use of violence by the colonial state to throttle Māori self-determination. It wasn't enough to arrest its leaders — the entire fact of the pā had to be erased. It took two weeks to tear down the houses and evict over a thousand people from their homes and a further two months to destroy all of Parihaka's cultivations. For a time, before its spiritual and physical reconstruction, the pā was left a wasteland, its leaders imprisoned without trial for sixteen months, its people scattered, and its bank, bakery and 250 or so whare raupō demolished.

Parihaka was invaded because it was potent: a powerful centre of Māori authority, autonomy and protest. It was not to do with the appropriation of land (you cannot confiscate for a second time something you have already taken). The intention was to bludgeon Māori into submission. Why otherwise would you destroy someone's gardens? Why destroy the very things that keep a people alive?

To Bryce and others, Tohu and Te Whiti's community threatened the legitimacy of the colonial state. The taking of the land was far from the least of it; but introducing pass laws, a rogue government arbitrarily suspending the rule of law, suppression of the press and the destruction of indigenous communities and their political structures: these are the acts of a government bent on annihilation. This is the conduct of an administration backed by '[t]he voice of the public [which] said, Extinguish Parihaka, the fountain of disaffection'.[52] We in Aotearoa have seen these things happen elsewhere and have been quick to criticise them. They happened here, too — and my great-grandfather was part of them.

He had joined the AC on 27 August 1877.[53] A decade earlier the Armed Constabulary Act had centralised various policing, detective and military functions in anticipation of the departure of imperial troops from the country (the last of whom had left by 1870). At peak strength it numbered nine divisions, including two comprising Māori constables, each containing sixty to eighty men (generally an inspector, two sub-inspectors, three sergeants, three corporals and sixty constables). The AC was, in essence, a heavily armed mobile police force, tasked with imposing the peace in 'disturbed' areas and helping to establish the conditions for settlement through the 'pacification' of Māori and the construction of roads, bridges and telegraphs and so forth.[54] Bluntly, its job was to 'impose the norms of the conqueror upon the conquered'.[55]

In its early phases the AC was an elite force comprising men who had survived an 'intensive culling process' and rigorous training, and who were supplemented by 'superior' recruits from other Australasian paramilitaries attracted by the pay and conditions.[56] Armed initially with old breech-loading carbines, the AC was later supplied with

Snider rifles, which were considered formidable weapons given the speed with which they could be loaded and fired. Early annual reports of the AC listed the results of marksmanship tests, although by the mid-1880s these had been replaced by detailed tables listing the incidence of criminal offences.[57]

By the time Andrew signed up, things had changed. For one thing, the country was heading into the long depression of the 1880s (so perhaps the prospect of steady work accounts for his decision). The effects of spending cuts were being felt across the public sector, and in the AC there was high turnover as well as discontent among the rank and file with low rates of pay (in Westland tradespeople earned nearly 30 per cent more than a basic constable) and the sorry state of facilities.[58] Life in the AC could be tedious, and if at any point Andrew sought light relief in the libraries the Constabulary maintained he would have been right out of luck, for the selection extended only to 'serious' novels, books of sermons, and other 'uplifting' literature.[59]

There was unhappiness, too, with administrative changes. In 1877 the Constabulary absorbed the police forces of the recently disestablished provinces, and the new entity was formally renamed the New Zealand Constabulary Force (although it continued to be known colloquially as the AC). The police and military wings were operationally distinct, but the amalgamation was not an easy one: there were tensions over rates of pay, transfers, promotions and dismissals.[60] All things considered, Andrew — who was in the military wing (known from 1883 as the Field Force) — chose an inauspicious year in which to join up.

The AC's records contain Andrew's registration number (796) and note that he was 5 feet 11¼ inches tall, had had no previous military service, was of 'fresh complexion' and had light brown hair and pale blue eyes. He may initially have been with the provincial police in Kumara on the West Coast of the South Island, but by mid-1880 he is in camp in Pungarehu, just a mile and a half from Parihaka pā.[61]

For a brief spell I felt compelled to pin down with absolute certainty that Andrew either was or was not part of the invading force on 5 November 1881, which heroically punched its way through lines of boys who 'danced splendidly', girls with skipping ropes and women carrying loaves of bread as gifts.[62] (The gifts of food did not stop: on New Year's Day 1882, mere weeks after their pā had been destroyed, Parihaka people prepared a hangi for the AC.) What I really wanted to establish, of course, was that he was *not* there. It was a way of avoiding the issue.

In my early correspondence with Archives New Zealand Te Rua Mahara o te Kāwanatanga they apologised for not having found anything that definitively placed Andrew at Parihaka. On reading that, part of me felt let off the special hook reserved for those whose forebears were members of a military force which invaded a village, raped women, looted taonga, destroyed hundreds of hectares of

The AC Coastal rugby team at the Rāhotu Domain in 1881. Andrew Gilhooly, the captain, is standing fourth from left in the back row, holding the ball.

crops, stole livestock, transported prisoners far away and introduced pass laws restricting Māori movements into, out of and within Parihaka long after the invasion.[63]

But of course that communication did not constitute proof that he was *not* at Parihaka. Four pieces of evidence convince me that he was. The first is a photo taken in 1881 in which Andrew is standing with fifteen other men (one of them the manager) who comprise the AC Coastal rugby team. The inscription indicates that he was the captain and that the photo was 'possibly taken at the Rahotu Domain', where Forster Goring's No. 3 Company was based, not far from Parihaka.

The second artefact is tucked away in the 11 June 1911 edition of the *Opunake Times*, where a small item places Andrew Gilhooly among the AC contingent that completed the South Road between Ōkato and Ōpunake in 1881. The third is the note scribbled by my Great-aunt Liz, which says that in the 1880s her father was 'manpowered to [the] Armed Constabulary — Pungarehu (Parihaka)'.

And the fourth — the smoking gun, if that is not an inappropriate choice of words — is found in Andrew's service record. He spent nine years in the AC, comprising three consecutive three-year periods of service. Having joined in 1877 he repeated the oath of allegiance to Her Majesty Queen Victoria at the AC's Cape Egmont camp on 8 September 1880, which suggests he was one of the forty-two constables deployed to protect the Cape Egmont lighthouse, which had been brought north from Mana

Island and reconstructed in August 1881.[64]

He reattested at the AC's Parihaka camp on 10 September 1883. By then No. 3 Company was the only AC presence left at Parihaka and had been so since the end of February 1882.[65] Andrew did not leave the pā until November 1884, at which time many of the restrictions imposed in 1881 (including on movement) remained in place, and so he would have been there to see Te Whiti and Tohu return from imprisonment in the South Island in March 1883. In short, my great-grandfather was at Cape Egmont and Parihaka for at least four years, and so I find it inconceivable that he was not part of the invasion and the subsequent destruction of the pā.[66] So there it is — I am right back on the hook. It is not the last one I will catch myself on.

Anyway, trying to establish my great-grandfather's precise whereabouts on 5 November 1881 is a form of evasion; a sneaky way of saying — without saying — that whatever happened at and after Parihaka, he had no part in it. Present or not (and on 5 November two small detachments of AC men were left to guard the camps at Pungarehu and Rāhotu), for nine years my great-grandfather was a member of the instrument of the colonial state that razed the pā, and to harbour a hope that he might not have been there on the big day is to rather miss the point. Michel Quoist — the French priest, theologian and author — skewers any such attempt at evasion perfectly: 'It matters not whether you are among those who hit or among those who watch, among those who perform or among those who let it happen. You are all guilty, actors and spectators.'[67]

I am still looking at photos of the AC at Parihaka, trying to pick him out. Still figuring out what sense to make of this connection to events which have become emblematic of the crushingly destructive effects of colonisation in Aotearoa. I do not think that such meaning as there is to be found lies in judging Andrew, because it seems to me that slicing the apportioning of shame into little individual-sized bits is also a type of avoidance. The only thing that would be generated by blaming Andrew is the sense of self-righteousness and absolution that comes from passing judgement on others. That is just another way of wriggling off the hook.

Instead, I can confront my own ignorance, until recently, of what occurred at Parihaka. Buchanan makes a powerful point: 'Forgetting is rarely innocent. People have to work hard not to know, not to recall, not to see, to be truly ignorant.'[68] She says this from the point of view of someone who had whānau at Parihaka. I had family there, too, but mine stood in the ranks of the invaders. So I read her words differently. The first sentence I entirely agree with. For many years it was a choice to forget (or at the very least not to engage with, which amounts to the same thing) Parihaka and its aftermath, one which meant I could avoid dealing with my origins on the Coast.

Actually, even that is not quite correct. To forget a thing you have to have learned it, and I never made much of an effort to do the learning in the first place. I was not totally ignorant of the bare facts — the day, the month, the year, the Dick Scott book, the song Tim Finn did with Herbs — but little more than that.

How much effort did it take not to know, though? Not much. For nearly five decades I found it easy to evade Parihaka. God knows there is no shortage of knowledge regarding te pāhua — books, articles, music, films, websites, documentaries, archives, government reports, posters, poetry and art — none of it very hard to lay your hands on. Late at night on 10 June 2021 I googled 'Parihaka' and had 224,000 hits, so it's difficult to avoid unless you want to. I did, and it took very little effort on my part to wander about in the 'dementia wing' of our colonial history, where I had the company of an awful lot of other people.[69]

It took establishing that my great-grandfather was there on the day for me to directly confront that comfortable ignorance. But there is no avoiding or misremembering the issue now. What were once vaguely abstract and hazy notions — things that happened in another time and to other people; things quite easily forgotten, really, or never learned at all — have become deeply personal. They have become truths that need to be told.

Before starting this book I had no idea about a lot of things, including just how long the military occupation of Parihaka lasted. No. 3 Company, under Major Forster Goring, had arrived at Parihaka from Ōpunake via camps at Ōpua, Kaikahu, the Waitaha stream (where the camp was known as Pukehinau) and Rāhotu.[70] It remained there — garrisoned in the Parihaka Redoubt (Fort Rolleston) overlooking the pā — until March 1885, when it was ordered back to Ōpunake as part of the new Stout/Vogel government's attempt at 'conciliation' with Māori.[71] As late as March 1884 it was still the largest garrison force in Taranaki, numbering two officers, five NCOs and fifty-four constables.[72]

The occupation was far from benign. On 17 April 1882 Goring's men broke up an attempt by 'Strange Natives — that is, Natives from different settlements within the Parihaka Block' to distribute food (including two dray-loads of pork) at the pā. Native Minister Bryce found the idea of Māori taking supplies to Parihaka to be 'in every way objectionable'. And so, in retaliation for 'this act of antagonism to the expressed orders of the Government' the AC pulled a dozen whare down — although Lieutenant Roberts thoughtfully ensured that 'everything [was] removed out of them first'.[73]

In the years that followed the invasion, Pākehā fears regarding Parihaka never fully subsided. In 1885 they flared up to such an extent that a formal report (*Alleged Threatening Attitude of the Parihaka Natives*

Towards Europeans) was tabled in Parliament.[74] It is an odd document. At one level it is a litany of trivial settler concerns: two red window blinds and one green one have been stolen from the property of Mr Thomas Wallace, along with 'other items of little intrinsic value'. Mr Driller had 'some little difficulty about pigs, when he says threats were used; but that is now all over, and he is the best of friends with the Natives'.

So, too, it seems, is one of my great-grandmother's half-brothers. In 1885, Fleming fences were once again the centre of attention when:

> a chief named Te Whetu with some of his tribe were getting in horses in the neighbourhood of Cape Egmont for sale, when some of them, by some means, got into Mr. Fleming's paddock, and to get them out the Maoris made a gap in the ditch-and-bank fence, instead of taking them out at the gate. I asked Mr. Fleming if he wished to prosecute the Maoris, when he replied that he did not, as the damage was so trifling, while he and Te Whetu were on the most friendly terms, and he did not wish anything to be done to break that friendship.[75]

But the report also conveys a deep-seated anxiety that 'a great change has come over the Natives of that district [which] puts me in mind of their manner during the ploughing matches and the Parihaka scare . . . If something is not done, I feel sure that we shall have a repetition of the Parihaka scare.' Māori are seen loitering; confrontations are taking place; threats are being made. Mr Elwin 'knows of no threats himself but his son-in-law has heard from a native that a king was coming from Waikato to head the Natives, who were to recover all the land back from Europeans, including the houses'.

The native officer is sent to inquire, and while he finds some evidence of 'threats and other annoyances', most of what has been reported is trifling and concerns 'ordinary criminal matter[s] [that] can have no political bearing'. But they do: Pākehā voices are raised, public meetings are called for and demands are issued that 'thirty or forty' constables be sent to Pungarehu. Immediately.

In the end, the authorities conclude that 'the whole scare has been got up by a few interested persons for their own individual ends, and is now being kept alive by them and a few fussy individuals through the Press'. But even if Pākehā alarm is exaggerated, there is something in this episode I find worth reflecting on. All of the events recounted in the 1885 parliamentary report take place after Goring's No. 3 Company left Parihaka. Clearly, at least some of the settlers feel exposed by the departure of the AC. Vulnerable. Perhaps they think they can hear the sounds of the ruru coming home to roost.

Putting things off

I would like to delay the reckoning just a little longer, though, the better to track Andrew during the few years that he was gone from the Coast, before he re-emerged on a farm located between Pungarehu and Rāhotu. What happened in the missing years is this. The AC remained in camp at Parihaka until May 1885, although Andrew was long gone by then, transferred to the East Coast on 26 November 1884 for a short stint and thence to the AC's Tapuaeharuru depot in Taupō in April of the following year.[1]

By this time the AC was winding down. In 1885 all of its bases in the Taupō–Tauranga district (with the exception of Wairoa) were closed, and Andrew and his comrades were put to work building roads at Tokaanu. (Fun fact: Taupō's AC Baths are named after the armed constables who built the original pool.) And when the AC was dissolved in 1886 he headed south to Port Chalmers to join the Permanent Militia.

There is a backstory to this. At around the time Andrew was building roads on the southern end of Lake Taupō, public and political debate had flared up regarding the construction of an artillery-based coastal defence system to protect against external threats (the internal ones — Tītokowaru, Te Whiti, Tohu and Te Kooti — having presumably been seen off by then).[2] That debate had bubbled away over previous decades. In 1885 war between Britain and Russia over the status of Afghanistan seemed inevitable, and it was feared the conflict would envelop the British Empire's colonies in the south Pacific.[3] It 'was well known', in fact, 'that a fully-equipped naval force was prepared and on the eve of starting on its tour of spoliation and destruction throughout the ports of New Zealand and Australia . . . [and] war with a powerful European nation was inevitable'.[4]

Separate engineering, torpedo and artillery units had been established in the military wing of the AC in the early 1880s, and by 1883 'many of the soldier-police were busily engaged in mounting guns at the four main ports'.[5] When the Constabulary was formally disbanded under the 1886 Defence Act, its policing and military functions were transferred to the New Zealand Police Force and the New Zealand Permanent Militia respectively. The infantry, engineers, torpedo and artillery corps shifted into the latter — the nation's first standing army — on 1 September 1886, and two months later my great-grandfather headed south to join No. 4 Battery in Dunedin.[6] On 8 December 1886, Andrew transformed himself from Constable A. Gillooly into No. 67 Bombardier A. Gillooly.

He spent just over four years at Port Chalmers, possibly working alongside convict labour on the construction of Taiaroa Head's lighthouse battery. He certainly served under the same Forster Goring who led No. 3 Company at Parihaka, and who also moved into the Militia's artillery corps when the AC faded away.

Then, in mid-February 1891, Andrew was reassigned to the garrison artillery's Wellington depot. Ill-health seems to have driven this move, because partway through that year he applied for discharge from the Permanent Militia with compensation. A supportive memo from his commanding officer, Captain Morrison, explains that Andrew has asked to leave because 'his eyesight has deteriorated so much that he cannot lay a Gun', an affliction attributed by a medical specialist to the heavy lifting of artillery pieces while he was down south.[7] Andrew also sustained long-term damage 'when discharging Defence Material' out on the Otago Heads, where he 'accidentally wrenched the spine of his Back' so badly that he was hospitalised for two months in late 1889.

The net effect of both conditions, the commanding officer of No. 4 Battery tells us, is that Andrew has been rendered 'unfit for earning his livelihood at anything where strength and activity would be required'. In fact, his doctor went so far as to suggest that 'lifting heavy weights would tend to increase the amount of his short sightedness'. Which makes his choice of future career as a farmer the more surprising.

On 30 September 1891 Andrew is discharged from the Permanent Militia on compensation of '7/3 per diem'. That very same day Captain Anderson, the defence storekeeper at Mount Cook in Wellington — who works in the building where some of Te Whiti and Tohu's ploughers were imprisoned on their way south, which is immediately across the road from the church in which Andrew's son Dick will be ordained forty-two years later, and in the same area in which my daughter Camille now works — is asked by the Defence Office to 'have a Long Service Medal engraved for No. 67 Bombardier Andrew Gillooly, New Zealand Permanent Militia', in recognition of his 'good character' and fourteen years of service since he enrolled in the AC in 1877. A month later Andrew is back on the Coast.

But something is wrong. Something has slipped. Across the entire military history I've just described, the name of the man I've been talking of has been spelt 'Gillooly', not 'Gilhooly'. There is an extra 'l' where there should be an 'h'. Perhaps you've already picked it up, but I am not aware of this until I read Captain Morrison's memo — and then for some reason the spelling leaps out at me. I return to the AC's Description Book, an excerpt from which I'd received weeks earlier — and there it is: 'Gillooly' where all along I'd been seeing 'Gilhooly' in the copperplate.

It's not a big thing, to be sure, and yet all of a sudden I worry that the man I've gone to such lengths to track down is not my great-grandfather. This man belongs in someone else's story. But although this looks like a gold-plated chance to get off any number of hooks, it is not an opportunity I wish to avail myself of. Andrew Gillooly has given me much to get my teeth into and I am not at all willing to let him go.

My daughter Camille calms me down. She is a professional archivist and comes across this sort of thing all the time. Contested spellings; misremembered details; names lost in translation through the slip of a bureaucrat's pen (which I suspect is what happened with Andrew's sister Bridget). My mother is the support act, recalling a conversation she had with a parish priest in Limerick when she and Dad were there years ago. On hearing her maiden name, the priest sighed that even the Irish clergy couldn't agree on how to spell 'Gilhooly'.

(This affliction spread — across the years Andrew's name is spelt Gillooly, Gilhooly and Gilhooley, the last of which was also sometimes given to his son, Dick, in photos from his time at Sacred Heart College in Auckland.)

Then, when reading Michael Frayn's *Headlong* I discover another missing 'h'. Frayn explains that no one seems able to decide whether or not the artist Pieter Bruegel's name should be spelt 'Bruegel' (as it usually is) or 'Brueghel' (as his son's was). And that calls to mind my own father, who, as noted earlier, was always known as Bob; the only evidence that Keith Shaw ever existed is to be found on his primary school certificate and on cheques, which until the end of his life Dad always signed 'K. Shaw'. We still don't know why. So I decide that if Bruegel can be Brueghel and Keith can be Bob, then Gillooly can be Gilhooly.

Anyway, when I take into account the descriptions of Andrew's physical appearance, the dates of his movements, the fact that there is no 'Gillooly, A.' on any of the electoral rolls from the region but there is a 'Gilhooly, A.', and the reference in his obituary to his days in the good 'old A.C. Force', the chances that I am talking about someone else's great-grandfather are vanishingly small. All things considered, I am sure that Andrew Gillooly and Andrew Gilhooly are the same man. Well, almost entirely: that misspelling has lodged the tiniest sliver of uncertainty into my mind.

Land

On 28 October 1891 the man formerly known as Bombardier No. 67 writes a letter to the under-secretary of defence asking him to consider boosting his daily compo from 7/3 to 7/6 a day. The letter is posted from Hastings, but the Pungarehu Post Office is given as a return address. By the early 1890s A. Gilhooly/Gillooly is back on the Coast, farming a piece of land just a few kilometres from Parihaka. The farm is immediately adjacent to the military road he had helped push through a decade earlier, which carried first the AC into Parihaka and then the farmers who 'settled' the land.

It is important to me to establish how he came to be on that farm and two others as well. To know when that land passed out of Māori ownership and was harnessed to others' histories. Figuring this out means going beyond the stories, genealogies and miscellany produced for family, school or church reunions. Those sorts of accounts are often richly textured and reveal a great deal about settler life on the Coast, but sometimes there is a whiff of amnesia to them.

They tell of ships arriving, of clearing the land, of enduring privation, of establishing families and of putting down roots. Early in the piece there will invariably be an origin sentence such as: 'My family arrived in Taranaki in 1883 and has been there ever since' or some such. But what came before those sentences almost always remains untold. History begins with the purchase of the family farm.

Putting together the story of the Gilhooly farms means gathering scraps and snippets from old wills, electoral rolls, the parliamentary record, historic land titles, cadastral maps, minutes of Māori Land Court meetings, documents held by the public trustee and the archival records of the Waitangi Tribunal Te Rōpū Whakamana i te Tiriti o Waitangi . . . and then trying to make sense of that bricolage. What emerges is not the deep story of the land — that one does not feature in the official record and is not mine to tell in any case — but it is a story nonetheless, the narrating of which is a necessary complement to the other, more wholesome stories to be told. Those are well and good, but none of them would take the form they do were it not for the land. So it is the land I need to hear from and about.

The formal details of the purchase of the first of the three Gilhooly farms are contained in a certificate of title signed by both the minister of lands and the governor of the colony on 13 November 1895: in return for payment of £350 my great-grandfather gained title to the 114 acres comprising Section 44 Block 12 of the Cape Survey District.

This discovery surprises me, because I had assumed that Andrew had been granted this land as a former member of the AC. Not so: rather, his certificate of title was granted under the 1892 Land Act, which dealt with the sale of Crown land (including confiscated land). I'm no expert on these matters but it seems that it was not granted under the Naval and Military Settlers' and Volunteers' Land Act 1891, which set out the arrangements for administering claims lodged by former military men who were entitled to grants of land for services rendered. I've trawled through the parliamentary record and Andrew's name is not on any of the lists of those whose claims for land were accepted, rejected or deemed ineligible. I'm pretty sure that this is because, rather than retire when he left the AC, Andrew continued his military career with the Permanent Militia: at least in 1886, land was offered only to those men who opted to fully retire.

In any event, although Andrew doesn't become the legal owner until 1895, I think he was on the land before then. The 1891 letter to the under-secretary of defence, and a brief reference in the local press in 1893 to a 'clearing sale of Mr Gilhooly's dairy stock' at Pungarehu (which, despite the heavy rain, had 'a very fair attendance'), suggest to me that he began farming shortly after leaving the militia in 1891.[1] Further, on the cadastral map of Block 12 hanging on my wall at home the words 'Sold D. P.' are jotted on Section 44, which I take to mean that at the time Andrew purchased the farm payment was deferred (perhaps until 1895).[2]

The last bit of evidence that he was on the land before 1895 appears on page seventeen of the 1893 electoral roll for the district of Egmont, where can be found elector 892: 'Gilhooly, Andrew, Pungarehu, settler, residential.' (They've spelt his name correctly, thank God.) The appearance of the word 'residential' means he had to have been living in the area for at least six months. In 1879 the vote had been given to all men over the age of twenty-one, so long as they had lived in the country for at least twelve months and in their electoral district for six, or had freehold title to property worth at least £25.[3]

Andrew didn't get full title to Section 44 until 1895, which explains why he qualifies to vote in the 1893 election on the basis of residency. For a short period anyway, he was once again a tenant farmer. Given his people's history in Ireland he would have known all about that — even if the farm he was shortly to own outright was many times larger than that on which he had been born.

Section 44 is on the seaward side of the South Road, smack in the middle of what were once Parihaka's best cultivations and part of the 10,000 acres of the Parihaka Block which the West Coast Commission had recommended be retained by the Crown.[4] It is also right on the South Road and therefore part of a strip of land which, had the construction of that road been correctly carried out, would probably not have been made available for purchase under freehold title (for reasons we get to shortly). In the event, when the road was completed it was found to be closer to the mountain (and Parihaka) than had originally been planned, meaning that 5000 *additional* acres of land on the seaward side of the road — including the 114 that Andrew gained title to — were conveniently available for settlement.[5]

Because of this, the West Coast Commission recommended that all the Parihaka 'cultivations, pa sites, burial and fishing places on the seaward side of the road should also be allowed to be kept' by Māori.[6] In the event, only 1509 acres 'and 2 roods' — divided into thirty-three separate grants — were handed back to Māori, including 'some but definitely not all of the paa sites, cultivations and urupa in this part of Taranaki'.[7]

I have a copy of the map for Cape Survey District Block 12. It was completed in 1881 and is worth a close look. One feature is the Cape Egmont Lighthouse. The lighthouse is not a neutral structure. Along with the construction of the road Andrew worked on and the installation of the telegraph (which by 1880 linked all of the AC's camps in the district), its erection was an important part of the military campaign that led to the invasion of Parihaka. Indeed, in 1880 the West Coast commissioners explicitly referred to the 'very great political effect [that] would now be produced upon the Natives throughout the coast if they saw the three things for which the government have [*sic*] so long

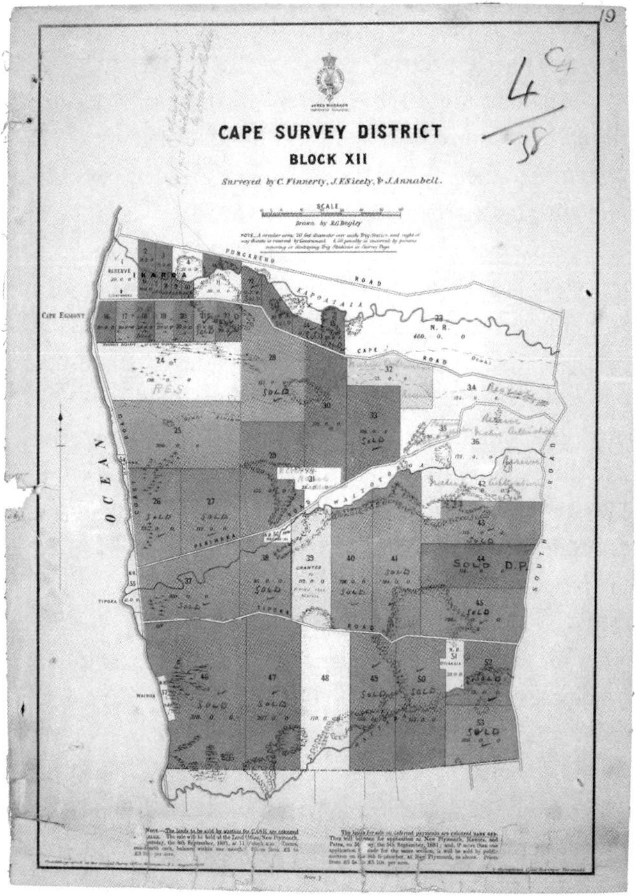

This map of Block 12 of the Cape Survey District dates from August 1881. Section 44, the first of the three Gilhooly farms, is adjacent to the South Road on the map's eastern side. Archives New Zealand Te Rua Mahara o te Kāwanatanga contended, being done together: the road, the telegraphy line, and the lighthouse'.[8]

A second feature of the map — one that casts back to the earlier actions of Te Whiti and Tohu's ploughers — is a reference to the £50 fine that will be 'incurred by persons removing or destroying Trig Stations or Survey Pegs'.

The third aspect that attracts my attention are those parcels of land that are coloured white. These are not for sale (not yet, anyway, although most of them soon will be). Section 1, for instance, on which the lighthouse stands, is a public reserve. (Within the wider Parihaka Block the Crown made provision for three gravel reserves, a police reserve, two recreation reserves and three education reserves.)[9] Most of them, however, are pieces of land that have been set aside for native reserves. A few of these are marked as 'native cultivations' — this was, after all, Parihaka's most fertile arable land.[10]

None looks remotely big enough to provide a viable economic base for hapū or iwi. Actually, most of them are *really* small — Sections 51, 54, 56 and 57 absurdly so. And some are shortly to disappear entirely. Look at Sections 34, 35, 36 and 42, which contain reasonably sized native cultivations. Now look carefully at the map of the Wairau and Cape Survey Districts, prepared some years later in 1898 (shown on the front endpapers of this book). The native reserves have been 'sectionised', carved into small parcels of land in preparation for sale to Pākehā farmers.[11] They have long since passed out of Māori ownership.

Those maps are framed and hanging on my wall, and as I gaze at them it becomes clear that the word 'map' is a weighty and powerful one. Maps are hard-working things whose job is to control space and give it meaning. They make some things visible and ensure that others vanish. The victors do not just write the histories — they also get to draw the maps. In doing so, they get to determine how the world is seen. In the case of the Taranaki maps the purpose is to impose Pākehā order on te ao Māori — to depict Taranaki as it should be (from a settler perspective) by converting uncharted territories where taniwha roam into tidy parcels of land on which Friesians and Jerseys will graze.

Little surprise, then, that you will find a road named after Stuart Newall on maps of the Taranaki coast. Newall was one of the AC officers involved in the arrest of Tohu Kākahi, Te Whiti o Rongomai and Hīroki at Parihaka, but he was also an experienced road builder who had surveyed the area south of the Hangatahua (Stony) River in 1880.

(Most of the attention given to the arrests that took place on 5 November 1881 rightly goes to Te Whiti and Tohu. But it is important not to forget the third man the AC marched away that day. Hīroki had killed a survey party's cook, John McLean, near the Waingongoro River in September 1878 and subsequently sought refuge at Parihaka. He was executed on 8 June 1882 at New Plymouth gaol and buried in an unmarked grave. In 1989 members of Taranaki iwi lifted the tapu that had been placed on the prison since Hīroki's death, and in 1994 his remains were exhumed and reburied at Parihaka.)[12]

Maps call some things into existence by destroying others. I try to imagine a map of the Parihaka area as it might have been conceived by Te Whiti and Tohu. I can't, of course, because that is beyond me on many different levels. But I'm pretty sure it wouldn't have had a surfeit of straight lines. And perhaps it would have been sketched by Te Kaahui Kararehe, the learned Parihaka scribe, writer, plougher and former South Island prisoner who advocated for his people in the Native Land Court, the High Court and the Court of Appeal, and who in 1885 built a small road through to Rāhotu known now as the Kahui Road.[13]

But on the maps on my wall the taniwha of Parihaka have been slain. A series of mostly straight lines denoting sections have been superimposed on land where Parihaka's cultivations once were. Even Māori reserves that once had names — Tarakihi, Ōkawa, Ikaroa, Te Putatuapo, Waitaraiti, Te Ngaue, Otuakaia — are reduced to numbers, sections and blocks. Rendered nameless and rubbed out of existence. The maps have done the political work of Bryce, Rolleston and the AC, slicing open the acres, roods and perches, obliterating the presence of Māori and erasing the history inscribed upon the land.

Granted, these are hardly original insights, but looking at those maps I see a connection that I was not previously aware of: just as Bryce wanted to control the people of Parihaka, so the survey maps serve to control their land.

If maps depict the resolution of contests of the imagination (as well as military campaigns), then when Te Ngaue becomes Section 4 Block 12 of the Cape Survey District it is pretty clear who has prevailed.

There is a tendency to treat Parihaka as if it is an 'invasion day story'.[14] The day of 5 November 1881 was certainly momentous, but focusing on that day alone obscures what happened over the long weeks, months and years that followed. Because Andrew's land had been retained by the Crown and was on the seaward side of the South Road he was able to buy his 114 acres outright. Had the South Road been further to the west, as originally surveyed, he would not have been able to do so, because around 20,000 acres of the Parihaka Block on the mountain side of the road were initially set aside for Māori reserves.

In fact, although the West Coast Commission had recommended that 25,000 acres on the eastern side of the South Road be returned to Te Whiti and his people, only 19,978 were handed back. Soon enough, the bulk of that land was either sold or leased to Pākehā farmers by the public trustee. The story of the leasing of land ostensibly set aside for Māori reserves is especially baleful, a form of 'bureaucratic violence' even less well understood than the military violence it followed.[15] I have a stake in this tale, too.

Briefly, in the mid-1860s the government gave an undertaking that some of the land it had confiscated in

Taranaki would be returned to hapū, including in the form of the native reserves. It finally got around to restoring some of that land to Māori in 1882. Outrageously, however, responsibility for the administration of these West Coast reserves was vested not with the Māori owners but in the hands of a government-appointed administrator, the public trustee, who was tasked with acting for the benefit of 'the natives to whom such reserves belong' *and* for 'the promotion of settlement'.[16]

These two requirements are fundamentally incompatible, and the nonsense of trying to reconcile them has long been recognised. As far back as 1907 a commission of inquiry pointed out that 'the concentration of control in a Department not in close touch with the Maori beneficiaries and their needs, whose paramount duty is to secure revenue from every part of the estate vested in it, is not always in the interests of the Maori beneficiaries, and is distasteful to them'.[17] Quite, and with good reason.

The second of the two imperatives under which the public trustee laboured has won out. By 1912 some 193,996 acres had been notionally set aside in reserves in Taranaki, but 120,110 (60 per cent) of them had already been leased to settlers by the trustee via twenty-one-year leases. And these were no ordinary leases: from 1887 they could be renegotiated without the approval of the land's owners, and from 1892 they came with a perpetual right of renewal, effectively (and quite literally) locking Māori out of their own land. (Little wonder 'the Natives [were] aggrieved at the [1887] innovation, which they consider detrimental to their interests.')[18] A further 18,400 acres were held under the same conditions but with thirty-year leases.[19]

There is more, as there always is. Quite apart from enjoying security of tenure, leaseholders could mortgage, sublet or transfer a lease to others. Under the Government Advances to Settlers Act 1894 they could also borrow money from the government to improve the land. Māori landowners could not (the clue is in the title of the act).[20] They were also forbidden from negotiating leases, and rents were systematically set by the public trustee at lower rates than would have been secured on an open market.

Moreover, after 1892 the trustee could also charge Māori to live on what remained of their own land. Some Māori owners paid more for these licences than some Pākehā farmers paid to lease Māori land. For example, in 1909 occupation licences for the Parihaka Reserve 'were set at between 2/6 and 5 shillings per acre per year [while] [t]he rate for the West Coast Reserves in the same area was between 1/6 and 2/6 per acre per year'.[21]

Unsurprisingly, this led to situations in which people who owned land that they could not live on sometimes found themselves in debt. There is a set of public trustee accounts (1902–4) concerning land that had been leased on the Waiotama Block. Five of the eight leased sections have a debit balance. In other words, 'even though the Public Trustee was leasing the land and the owners could not occupy it, they were getting into debt . . . The costs that were charged that caused this debt included: survey fees, Crown and Native Land rates, costs for bushfelling, the 7.5 per cent commission that the Public Trustee charged, land tax, interest on the overdrafts, the cost of the road and the cost of advertising the leases.'[22]

I struggle to get this straight in my head. This is land that is owned by Māori but controlled by the state, which is leased out at rates that are decided through a process the owners can play no part in, and which incurs debt over which those owners have little or no control, in part because they cannot live on and work their own land. Here, too, is something I found tucked away in a powerful little document prepared for the Waitangi Tribunal's Taranaki hearings:

> The total income from West Coast Leases for the period from December 1909 to December 1912 (three years) was 587 pounds and 7 shillings. Of this 64 pounds and 12 shillings and 10 pence was actually paid out to beneficiaries and a further 275 pounds and 17 shillings and 9 pence remained unpaid. It is not clear if this was withheld by the Public Trustee for some reason of [*sic*] if people refused to receive it. This means that during this three years the total income to the people who owned the land was 64 pounds from the entire 9,974 acres.[23]

Paltry returns. Rents withheld. Administration costs charged against (paltry) revenues. Being told where you could and could not live on your own land — and then paying for the privilege of doing so. If this is not clear enough, a letter written in 1909 by the public trustee to the chair of the parliamentary Native Affairs Committee lays bare the racism Māori landowners were up against: 'The average condition of the native is still far from satisfactory and pending an all round improvement they must be considered as not yet satisfactorily advanced to control the reserves provided for them.'[24] Somehow, he (I feel safe in assuming it's a he) has managed to completely miss the rich Māori gardens and cultivations on the Coast, which is not a bad effort as they're even marked on the bloody cadastral maps of the time.

Four years later the trustee sends a rambling, bizarre letter to the people of Parihaka berating them for their stewardship of their own land:

> There is a law relating to noxious weeds applying to pakeha and Maori alike. It is that the owner and occupier of land must keep the land clear of all weeds or he is liable to not obeying this law. Maoris have not been fined yet, but they will be in the future or else they will suffer the other penalty ie they will run the risk of losing possession of their lands. It is necessary for the welfare of all the people, Maori and Pakeha alike, that all lands should be made productive of wealth. The race for supremacy among the nations is becoming so keen that the British supremacy on the seas will be challenged unless further strength is added to the Empire's defence by an increase in

the ships of war. This is the only manner in which we can feel assured that our country will not fall into the hands of an enemy.

We shall not be able to sustain an increased navy and the other burdens of Government unless we cause the land to produce more wealth. For these reasons, it is necessary that all lands should be brought into cultivation.

At the present time the Maoris of Parihaka are enjoying many of the advantages of the progress of civilization in Aotearoa without in any way bearing the burdens of it. This is especially so in regard to the question of roads, as the Parihaka Maoris have contributed very little as rates to the Road Boards.[25]

It's impressive, don't you find, in a deeply dysfunctional manner? Not only are the people of Te Whiti and Tohu receiving peppercorn rents and paying to live on their own land (having previously 'enjoyed the advantages of the progress of civilisation' in the form of the confiscation of their land and the destruction of their pā), they are also charged with imperilling the safety of the realm by not ripping out noxious weeds such as gorse, ragwort and blackberry — most or all of which had been introduced by Pākehā. By turn racist, incoherent, hectoring, haranguing, threatening, cajoling, hysterical and historically ignorant — and all this from the holder of a public office who has a statutory obligation to act for the benefit of 'the natives to whom such reserves belong'.[26]

The depth of the hostility towards Māori is breathtaking (but only if you are encountering it for the first time, I imagine), and I have trouble getting it into human-sized perspective. Once more Te Miringa Hohaia, Marlene Benson and Rachel Buchanan help me out, recounting a small story in the context of the much bigger one of the long bureaucratic strangulation of the relationship between Māori and their land.[27]

In 1887 some 18 acres at the northern end of the 50-acre reserve on which the Cape Egmont Lighthouse stands were leased from the Marine Department by a Parihaka leader, Te Whetu Moeatu (a close friend of Te Kaahui; the men had been born on the same day).[28] Over the years, the leaseholders made a number of offers to buy the land from the department, all of which were rebuffed. On the other hand, repeated attempts by officials and local farmers to prise the land away from the leaseholders eventually succeeded in the early 1950s. In the end, it was pretty straightforward.

The then-leaseholder, Mrs Louie Okeroa, came into the New Plymouth office of the Lands and Survey Department to arrange the new lease that the Marine Department had agreed to offer her. The official sitting behind the desk — clearly of one mind with the field officer for the commissioner of Crown lands, who 'was not very enthusiastic to lease [that particular land] to a Maori' — refused to allow her to sign the lease and pay for it.[29] With 'the rent unpaid and lease unsigned, the land was subsequently surveyed and sold to Pākehā farmers'.[30] Simple as that.

Here in Aotearoa we are terribly enthusiastic about treating people equally. But Mrs Okeroa was not dealt with in the same way a Pākehā leaseholder would have been. Equal treatment was similarly found wanting in a draft of what became the Native Lands Administration Act 1886, which suggested that, 'Although great benefit is likely to be derived from the uniting of the Europeans and Maoris, it is not yet clear that the laws should apply equally to both races at the present time, as it is uncertain how the Natives would be able to support themselves.' (It becomes tricky to support yourself when your land has been taken from you.)

Equal treatment was not a conspicuous feature of the Native Land Settlement Act 1907 either. In the interests of opening up 'surplus' Māori land for settlement, the legislation 'gave the Maori Land Boards the ability to compulsorily vest "unutilised" Maori land in themselves, and required [Māori landowners] to sell half the vested land'.[31] Too bad if those owners 'might have children who would be their successors and to whom the land would be necessary for occupation when they became of age'.[32]

Can you imagine that rule being applied to Pāhekā? Robert Stout and Apirana Ngata could, pointing out that '[i]f, therefore, the Maoris as freeholders are not to be permitted to lease their lands when they desire to do so, but are to be forced to sell half of the land they desire to lease, the same law must be applied to Europeans'.[33] It wasn't, of course.

Then there is the Maori Affairs Act 1953, which for years allowed Māori land to be sold even though not all of the owners might be present at or even notified of meetings held to discuss and decide on such sales. It also allowed for sales to go through when owners who were present at the meetings objected. All of this 'is legal under present and past legislation, [but] none of these things can happen during sales of land other than Maori land'.[34]

And finally, equal treatment was certainly not the lot of Māori members of the Ōkato parish in the early twentieth century. In a 1921 letter to the head of the Roman Catholic Church, Archbishop O'Shea, the local priest mentions that Māori parishioners will attend Christmas Day Mass at 11 p.m. while 'the Whites' will come along for the traditional midnight Mass.

This is what institutional racism looks like: banal, bureaucratic and incremental. Just the ways things are. No overt physical violence needed. But the devastating effects of this regime were and are experienced daily:

> [A]s each generation of Maori succeeded to lands they could never walk on, they inherited the history of war, protest, imprisonment, and dispossession. They succeeded not only to lands under perpetual leases but to the perpetual reminder of forced alienation . . . [and were] denied even the right to forget. How could they forget

> when they saw their children leave home to seek work while they knew that the family land down the road would always be worked by strangers? How could they ask their children to respect the law and the property of others when they knew, and their children knew, that by the same law their own property had been permanently taken from them?[35]

Singer/songwriter Aldous Harding might call this 'the weight of the planets' bearing down on Māori.[36] I imagine that Mrs Okeroa certainly felt the weight of the planets on her shoulders the day she returned home from the Lands and Survey Department. But I suppose it is not for me to speculate on how the farmer or the bloke from the Lands and Survey Department might have felt.

One of the reasons it is not my place to do so is because my ancestors also benefited from the West Coast lease system.[37] I have known for years that, in addition to the original farm, Kate and Andrew had two others, both on the mountain side of the South Road; it began to dawn on me that they had likely been on land set aside for Māori reserves and subsequently leased to Pākehā farmers by the public trustee.

Eventually I started piecing together their stories. Back down the historic rabbit holes, around the wrong turnings and along to the dead ends; hours in the company of a magnifying glass trying to decipher highly pixellated digital versions of faded documents written in barely decipherable copperplate; following faint leads through the institutional networks of Archives New Zealand Te Rua Mahara o te Kāwanatanga, the Waitangi Tribunal Te Rōpū Whakamana i te Tiriti o Waitangi, the Taranaki Research Centre Te Pua Wānanga o Taranaki and Toitū te Whenua Land Information New Zealand. Scraps here; bits and pieces there; good and helpful people everywhere.

As the fragments began to come together, it became clear to me that not only do my roots stretch back to the invasion of Parihaka and to confiscated land on the seaward side of the South Road, they also extend into West Coast leasehold land.

You reach one of these farms if you head a mile up the Opourapa Road towards the mountain.[38] Section 2 Block 13 of the Cape Survey District was part of the Waiotama Block, which was sandwiched between the Parihaka reserves to the north and the Opourapa Road to the south. Waiotama comprised 1895 acres, which the Crown granted to Whareuanui and forty-five others in 1882, specifying — as it typically did — that the grant was 'absolutely inalienable'.[39] It was nothing of the sort, of course.

Control of the land was quickly vested in the public trustee, and from 1894 parcels were being leased to farmers. By 1908, 75 per cent of the 'absolutely inalienable' block had been leased under perpetually renewable twenty-one year leases. No record has been found of any discussions or meetings between the Māori owners and the public trustee about those leases, whose effect has often been to absolutely alienate Māori from their land in perpetuity.[40]

For some time I was unsure when Andrew and Kate first set foot on the Opourapa Road farm. I have a sense that they were there by 1902, because on 20 May that year my great-grandfather complained to the *Opunake Times* that a roading contractor working on the Opourapa Road — a Mr Thrush — was 'throwing trees across his [Andrew's] fencing line'. And a year later, the same newspaper reported that he was lobbying the Parihaka Road Board — which at that time may well have been chaired by his brother-in-law, Michael Fleming — 'asking that steps be taken to raise a special loan of £1,400 for forming and metalling' the Opourapa Road.

The hunch solidifies when, sifting through Hohaia and Benson's forensic history of the alienation of the Parihaka Block, I happen across evidence that in 1902 Section 2 Block 13 was leased by the public trustee for £35 per year, and that it has remained West Coast leasehold land ever since, transferred in 1977 to Parininihi ki Waitotara (which in 1976 had taken on the administration of the 55,000 or so remaining acres of leasehold land).[41]

The final piece of the Opourapa Road puzzle thuds into place, and suspicions are duly confirmed, when I receive a copy of a document signed by my great-grandfather on 6 January 1922, just a year before his death, which renews the lease he took out on Section 2 Block 13 under the West

Coast Settlement Reserves Act 1892. Several details stand out. The first is that the rent has increased from £35 to £47 per year, payable in twice-yearly instalments. The lease makes clear that, should Andrew stumble upon 'mines, metals, minerals, coal, lignite, slate or freestone' in the process of milking his cows, ownership of those resources shall remain with the native trustee.

Andrew gives a solemn undertaking that he will paint all wooden constructions on the property every four years; keep the premises in a 'clean and husbandmanlike' fashion; ensure that 'all live hedges and fences' are properly cut and trimmed (and that the dreaded gorse, which looms large in farmers' nightmares, does not spread); and maintain all fences to the level demanded by the Fencing Act 1908 (which may explain his run-in with Mr Thrush). It goes without saying that the lease is perpetually renewable. There is no sign, mention or indication whatsoever of the land's owners.

So there it is. One farm purchased outright in 1895 and a second leased in 1902 under the West Coast lease regime. Both on confiscated land. One to go.

The story of the third farm — Section 102 Block 12 of the Cape Survey District, the land on which my mother spent her early years and which was directly opposite Andrew and Kate's original property — is brief and blunt and goes like this. In 1916 the Native Land Court amalgamated the Te Upokomutu, Ngātirangitumamao, Ngātimoeahu and Parihaka Kāinga blocks into a single consolidated Parihaka Block. As part of that process Section 102 Block 12 was partitioned into Parihaka A, a southern section of 103 acres, and Parihaka B, which was a smaller northern piece of just 36 acres. Ownership of the first was vested in Hori Teira, who also had to pay for an occupation licence to live on the property, while Rihikau was acknowledged as the owner of the smaller parcel.[42]

On 31 August 1921, not long before Andrew died, Teira sold 98 acres' worth of Parihaka A to my great-grandmother for £2947. Not to Andrew, as I have always thought was the case, but to 'Kate Gilhooly of Pungarehu, Married Woman'. The Aotea District Māori Land Board identifies Kate as the sole owner of the land. Two slivers were excluded from the sale: an urupā, which remained in Māori hands, and a small slice that was added to another title.

That is how the land that became Kate's farm was alienated and Europeanised. I don't use these terms deliberately to provoke. 'Alienation' and 'Europeanisation' were formal descriptions used by the Native Land Court to describe the process through which West Coast reserve land ceased to be Māori land. Sometimes the sales didn't go through, and as you browse through the records you stumble across the chilling phrase 'Europeanisation deferred'. (For the time being.)

But much more often than not they did. Here is just one example from hundreds. In September 1902 the court authorised the sale of Pungaereere, a piece of land near Ōpunake. The particulars are recorded in 'Alienation file

8/155/1/1' and the 'Area alienated' was the whole block. There were also 'alienors' who did the selling and 'alienees' who benefited from the alienation. The language is deliberate and communicates the permanent severance of the link between Māori and the land.

The man from whom my great-grandmother purchased Parihaka A has his own niche in this story, as well as in the histories that have been written of Taranaki. Hori Teira, who appears as the 'part European George Taylor (Hori Teira)' in Dick Scott's *Ask That Mountain*,[43] was born in Kororāreka in 1845 to a Ngāti Ruanui woman, Ngāurupa, and an Englishman, John Taylor.[44] Teira's mother, who had been taken north by Waikato iwi following the Musket Wars and then further north still by missionaries, brought him home from the Bay of Islands as a young boy.

In September 1862 he was among those who, under the leadership of Wiremu Kīngi te Matakātea and Te Whiti, helped shipwrecked passengers from the *Lord Worsley* make their way from the beach at Te Namu, near Ōpunake, to New Plymouth — on condition that each passenger 'pay a toll of 5s at the Maori toll-gate at Kapoaia [*sic*] as an acknowledgment that they were traversing Maori country'.[45]

Hori Teira was one of the toll collectors at the gate located at Te Ikaroa a Maui, near Kapoaiaia. At the time the tariff for a minister of the Gospel was £50 while a 'Maori disciple of the Governor' paid £200: a Pākehā policeman paid the top rate of £500 — as did anyone carrying a letter 'badly tempting the tribe'.[46] (For a Māori policeman, which Hori Teira would in time become, the toll was set at £5.) In general, Māori did not pay a toll, but they were asked to contribute one pence if 'things [were] carried on a man's back'.[47]

Teira also helped a certain Mr Graham — the member of the House of Representatives for Franklin who, shortly after the shipwreck, would also become the superintendent of the province of Auckland — get hold of a horse which was then used to transfer several boxes of gold (worth £12,000) from the ship to New Plymouth. For Graham this was the second shipwreck in fairly short order: earlier, on his way south to attend the first sitting in Wellington of the colony's general assembly, he had also been shipwrecked off Castlepoint.[48]

The following year Hori Teira was part of a warrior party that ambushed a contingent of British Army soldiers at Wairau, near Tataraimaka, in the first action of the Second Taranaki War. Some days prior he had sustained a wound to one of his hands while working in the bush and had sought assistance from Dr William Astle Hope, an Irish surgeon from County Wicklow who had joined the 57th (West Middlesex) Regiment in 1858.[49] The 57th called themselves 'The Die-Hards': they had arrived from Bombay in July 1860 and by 1863 were based at the Tataraimaka (St George's) Redoubt.

Nine men were killed at Wairau on 4 May 1863, including Lieutenant Hope.[50] It seems that Teira claimed a watch, chain and ring from Hope's body, but, rather than give the objects away, as was Taranaki custom following the killing of a foe in a warrior's first battle, he held on to them.

Three weeks later, on 29 May, Hori Teira was captured following a second skirmish with members of the 57th, this one near the regiment's former camp at Poutoko Redoubt, just to the south of New Plymouth. Curiously, although he was shot at close range with a revolver, no mark of a bullet was subsequently found on him. What *was* found on him, however, were Hope's possessions. Assumptions were made and conclusions drawn, as they are, and Hori Teira was tried for and convicted of the surgeon's murder (as well as for shooting with intent and receiving stolen goods) and sentenced to death.[51]

Teira's conviction for murder looked decidedly off. For one thing, Hope was killed in a military action — and Teira was not alone in questioning whether a charge of murder could be brought during a state of war. Further, no one seemed clear that Teira was the one who had pulled the trigger. The coroner's jury found that Hope had been '[c]ruelly and barbarously murdered by certain persons of the Native Race to the jurors unknown'. In fact, on 15 July the *Otago Daily Times* reported that the jury had initially been inclined to recommend mercy (although it does not explain how mercy became execution). And as Teira himself would later point out, in the melee 'how could a man tell which of the forty of us killed any of those men?'[52]

Nevertheless, the sentence stood. Hori Teira was

awaiting execution in Auckland's Mount Eden prison when he was informed that his sentence had been commuted following the intervention of the new superintendent of Auckland, who had 'rejoiced in the opportunity of repaying the kindness' Teira had extended him following the shipwreck of the *Lord Worsley*.[53] Graham had personally petitioned Governor George Grey, whose sanction was required before the hanging could be carried out. Grey agreed that Teira's act was one of warfare rather than murder and commuted the sentence to life imprisonment with hard labour.

Four years later Hori Teira was freed and, following a period working on Graham's Ladies Mile property in Auckland and his gold claim in Thames, returned to Taranaki. He was prevailed upon by the Taranaki land purchase officer, Robert Parris, not to return to Parihaka. In 1875 Teira became a native policeman and later a member of the AC, in return for which he was granted 140 acres of land near Pungarehu.[54] He was initially based in Ōpunake, but when the AC began to gather in force around Parihaka, where his mother, brother and a significant number of his whānau lived, he successfully appealed to the minister of defence to be transferred to Pukearuhe, some 90 kilometres to the north.

For many Pākehā, what occurred at Wairau came to define Hori Teira — just as Teira himself, through the various accounts he offered of the events of 4 May 1863, significantly affected what is known of them. But he is important well beyond what occurred at and after Wairau. Through his relationship with James Cowan, in particular, Hori Teira had an influence on the Pākehā histories of those times.

Cowan, whose work significantly shaped perceptions of the New Zealand Wars in the early to mid-twentieth century, saw clearly that 'most of the printed narratives [of the wars] deal chiefly with events which came within the soldier-writers' own experience, and other contributions to the story of the campaigns are scarcely written in the impartial spirit of the historian'.[55] In an attempt to rectify that imbalance, Cowan's own histories drew on Māori sources (written and oral), and he acknowledges both Te Whiti and Hori Teira as among his 'principal Maori authorities' on the Taranaki wars, and in particular on Māori methods of military campaigning during those conflicts.

Four more things about this fascinating man. First: when Tuhiata confessed to the murder of Forster Goring's sister-in-law Mary Dobie in 1880, the confession was made in te reo Māori to 'one of his guards at the [Ōpunake] redoubt, Constable George Taylor, who was part-Māori'.[56] Next: in October 1897 Hori Teira's Pungarehu farm had its fences removed by two men and two women from Parihaka in an action that marked the beginning of a second campaign by Parihaka's ploughers. Third: while the Pākehā press often called on him for a 'native's view', following his death in 1935, at the age of ninety, the press reports erased that identity by describing him as a settler. And the last thing: some of my mum's generation grew up believing that Hori Teira lies in the urupā on the land he sold to 'Kate Gilhooly of Pungarehu, Married Woman'.

Except he doesn't. In fact, Hori Teira is buried in the Ōpunake cemetery.[57]

When I read through the details of Kate's purchase from Hori Teira, late one night, it felt as if something inside my head slipped its moorings — and not at all in a good way. Perhaps it shouldn't have. After all, unlike the Opourapa Road farm I haven't found any indication that Kate's land had been part of the pernicious West Coast lease system. The year she bought her farm from Hori Teira two adjacent sections were also transferred into Crown ownership, both subject to twenty-one-year leases with a perpetual right of renewal. On Kate's certificate of title, however, there is no mention of pre-existing leases.

All the same, for three reasons things seem to emotionally unravel. The first concerns the urupā. The only mention of the presence of someone's tūpuna on the land Kate purchased in 1921 is in the Land Board's paperwork, but that single reference ramps things up for me. Whose people were they? Did anyone tend them? Was the soil in which they lay fenced off from the cows? I have no answers to these questions, but between them my mother and her cousin Marie Leslie do.

Mum recalls that as kids they were forbidden from playing near the urupā. Marie, who spent longer on Parihaka A than Mum did (her father Tom, Kate's youngest son, purchased the farm from his mother's estate following Kate's death), recalls the urupā clearly. It was fenced off from the stock on a small rise they knew as Taylor's Hill — so called because (as far as Marie recalls) it holds the graves of members of the Taylor family.

The second reason the story of Section 102 shakes me is because there is an older land title — preceding the 1916 granting of the land to Hori Teira — indicating that Parihaka A had once been part of the larger Upokomutu Block. In October 1883 that land had been granted as a reserve to Te Whiti, Tohu and sixty-five other Māori. Minutes from sittings of the Māori Land Court (which was decidedly not a *Māori* court but part of the colonial state's judicial system) indicate that Hori Teira contested this grant: in October 1887 he can be found before the court arguing that 'Eruiti [*sic*] Te Whiti and [indistinct] John had no right to be in this grant'.[58] The presiding judge, Mr Rennell, respectfully disagrees, pointing out that the two men in question 'are placed at the head of the family by the West Coast Commission'.[59]

Rightly or wrongly, the evidence of an association between the men most closely associated with Parihaka and my great-grandmother's farm means that for me it is every bit as unquiet as it would have been were it leasehold land. Perhaps more so. This land whispers of people of power and times that are ancient, reaching much further back than 1916 or 1921.

The third is the name allocated to the land: Parihaka A. The farm my great-grandmother buys from Hori Teira, which was once on land granted to Te Whiti o Rongomai (but which in fact was controlled, leased and converted into Crown land by the public trustee), is the very first piece of land listed in the historical documents that set out in remorseless detail the alienation of the Parihaka Reserve. Pākehā authorities presumed to give the land my mother ran on as a child, and which is part of my history, a Māori name that contains multitudes. The weight — not of the planets, but certainly of the obligation to absorb, reflect and in some way act on this knowledge — quietly settles upon me.

One last thing about those two farms. In 1882 the Crown decided to hold back 5000 acres from any future reserves as 'an indemnity for the loss sustained by the government in suppressing the . . . Parihaka sedition'.[60] The sedition that was pacific and non-violent, and whose protagonists welcomed my great-grandfather and his AC comrades into the pā with gifts of food. Those 5000 acres lay between the Waiweranui Stream and the Newall Road in the north, and the Ngariki Road and the Ōpunake Block in the south.[61] They included Andrew's Opourapa Road farm and Kate's Section 102 Block 12 of the Cape Survey District.

I have found enough coordinates to navigate the set pieces of Andrew's life, but have had less success uncovering evidence of the ebb and flow of the daily life he and Kate led on the coast. There are no letters and few photos. There are, though, several newspaper reports featuring Andrew (although none in which Kate appears), from one of which it is clear that his farming career got off to a rough start. Someone once suggested of former members of the AC that 'the Irish would-be farmers at least were excellent diggers and if not used to sheep, as were Scots, knew pigs and cattle and horses'.[62]

That optimistic assessment appears not to have applied to Andrew, because when Newton King, a well-known Taranaki stock agent, held his clearing sale on Andrew's farm in late 1893 he found that 'several of the cows were backward, and nearly all [were] in low condition'.[63] But Andrew must have learned his craft (perhaps by reaching back into his own past), because by 1915 the same Mr King is happily reporting the sale of 'a very prime Shorthorn cow fattened by Mr A. Gilhooly of Pungarehu'.

I learn from these old paper clippings, too, that my great-grandfather was a member of the Rahotu Athletics Club and the Pungarehu school committee, and that in 1895 he helped 'supply the music' at the annual district bachelors' ball (playing a violin that he passed on to his eldest son, my grandfather Hugh), where the 'refreshments were all that one could wish for' and the dancing 'commenced punctually at 8 p.m. and did not break up until nearly 4 a.m.'.

(Little surprise that his cows were backward.)

In 1901 he won first place in the Rhubarb section of the Farm and Garden Produce division of the Cape Egmont Horticultural Society's 3rd Annual Show. A year later he took out the first prize for Ham, but in 1903 he returned to the Rhubarb contest in which he could do no better than second. And in 1904 he impounded a three-year-old heifer that had been wandering on his land and whose ears had 'apparently been bitten by dogs'. It is all very bucolic and feels a long way from the AC and No. 4 Artillery. In fact (and I'm aware that I'm muddling my senses when I say this), when I read those old newspapers what I hear is the sound of silence building around Parihaka. It is already being forgotten.

Andrew died in the New Plymouth public hospital on 6 February 1923 and was buried in the Ōkato cemetery. He was sixty-six and had remained a British national. There is a grim irony to the fact that a man who was part of the invading force at Parihaka and who farmed on confiscated land died on what we now celebrate as Waitangi Day. A brief obituary in the *Opunake Times*, published a week after his death, tells us that out at Ōkato Andrew's pallbearers were all 'old A.C. Force comrades', one of whom, Jas Higgins, who had been a bugler with the Patea Rifles, played the 'Last Post'.

(In 1885 Higgins had come to the attention of the Resident Magistrate's Court for his role in a dispute over stolen stones — no, I have no idea either — but by 1923 he was a reformed character, serving as the area's poundkeeper. And unlike Andrew, Higgins did lodge a claim for a Crown grant of land — unsuccessfully, because he had not served the five years of continuous service that was required in order to qualify.)[64]

Higgins is beside the point. The point is that on a fine day that cemetery has a glorious view of Taranaki. In her meditation on what it takes to make a meaningful apology Rachel Buchanan explains that to this day there are Taranaki Māori who will not set foot on their maunga for the shame they feel at its loss, as well as that of their land, language and leaders in the 1860s.[65] Imagine that. I've tried and I can't, because the loss is not mine to bear. But the legacy of its perpetration? That is another matter.

In time the cows were dried off, then sold off, as was the land. My mum and most of her people have long since moved away from the Coast, but our origin story will always lie there. (As do many of our dead, especially at Ōkato.) 'The Coast' is as much a state of mind as it is a place, and both exert a powerful pull. I have only spent one year of my life there (when I was eight or nine we lived briefly in Ōpunake) and have seen from the road but never set foot on the Gilhooly farms.

Yet it is unquestionably where I come from: the ghosts and the histories and the memories and the stories and the characters and the landmarks and the living and the dead and the sheer *weight* of the Coast have collectively tethered me to it. It is a place of power and I could not disentangle myself from it even if I wished to, and I don't.

That land is where it began for us — and ended for others. It is where Dick is born. It is the foundation on which my mum's father establishes himself as a public figure through long years of membership of the Taranaki Hospital Board and the Taranaki Rugby Football Union. It is the place where my mother grew up and from where she sought to escape, meeting my father in the process. It is the place she went back to and where she had her first child, my sister Barbara. And it is still the place I take her out to see when I visit her in New Plymouth — driving along the war road my great-grandfather helped build and which carried the force that invaded Parihaka.

I cannot begin to imagine the despair that must be felt by Taranaki Māori who drive on that same road past that same land each day — exiles in their own country — and wonder what might have been had the colony's government kept its word and obeyed its own laws. Political commentator Emma Espiner points out that looking is not neutral — and I don't doubt that what I see as a landscape is seen by others as a 'traumascape' in which the past is never over.[66] 'The result of the Crown confiscation of the land of the Parihaka Block and subsequent government policies and actions since [is that] only 5,100 acres or 11% of the whole Parihaka Block remain[s] in Maori ownership today, 128 years later. Of this 2,000 acres or 5% is still held under perpetually renewable leases and so is not available for the use or occupation of the land's owners.'[67]

The last sale of confiscated land on the Parihaka Block took place in 1984.[68]

There is a coda to this, another small story nested within a larger one. In an old photo album of Mum's there is a newspaper article, written in 1981 to mark my Great-aunt Liz's reception of the Pro Ecclesia et Pontifice medal and scroll for outstanding services to the Roman Catholic Church as a choir mistress. In the report Liz, who was twin to Tom and lived with her mother Kate and sister Moll on Parihaka A, remembers going to monthly gatherings at Parihaka. Elsewhere, in a booklet prepared for the 1991 centennial of the Pungarehu School and District, Liz also refers to the 'special Maori Celebrations' held at the pā on the eighteenth of each month at which 'the Chan Māori Songs were memorable'.

I haven't the slightest idea what those songs were, but meetings had been held at Parihaka since the late 1860s to mark the day British troops fired the opening salvo at Waitara in the First Taranaki War. By the 1870s those events were attracting as many as 4000 Māori from across the country. They continued after the invasion of the pā. A decade or so after the AC marched in and tore the place down Parihaka had once again become one of the most well-developed villages — Māori or non-Māori — in the country, complete with electricity and water systems that put those of the capital city to shame, and large numbers of fascinated Pākehā would attend the monthly assemblies.[69] The gatherings, the rā, are still taking place on the eighteenth and nineteenth of each month when, as it always has, Parihaka welcomes those who wish to listen and learn about its past, present and future.

Interlude

Andrew's story, as far as I am able to tell it anyway, is indistinguishable from that of the colonisation of the Coast. I cannot tell it apart from the larger ones of Parihaka, land confiscation and the full-throttled assault by the colonial state on Māori political autonomy. He makes no sense to me without the tectonic changes he played a part in. His son Dick's tale, however, takes place in an entirely different world — one of schools, seminaries and Roman universities. There is no mention of confiscations, perpetual leases or ropey land purchases.

No mention of Māori at all, in fact. Dick is from an era when the events his father was embroiled in had already begun to sink into the realm of the unspoken, the untold and the unremembered — for Pākehā, although certainly not for Māori. So forgive me if you find that the tone goes 'clunk' every so often in the pages ahead. When that happens, and it will, it is because this account is moving now into a time when Parihaka was forgotten. You get used to it.

Kate

Before Dick, though, there is Kate. This book may be about some of the men in my life, but for a couple of reasons my great-grandmother is not a woman to be ignored. Again, the bare bones, which are all that remain of Catherine Fleming, get things started. Kate was born in Annah, Galbally, in County Limerick. (Kate and Andrew's villages are only 20 kilometres apart, but they met and married in a country 22,000 kilometres away from both.) She was one of seven children from her father Richard's second marriage, to Mary Hennessey, four of whom migrated with him to Aotearoa in 1895, joining several brothers and half-brothers who were already here.

My great-grandmother was four years old when her mother died at the age of thirty-seven, a fortnight after the birth of her final child. (Baby Johanna was raised by her half-sister Margaret, herself the last child of the marriage between Mary Mullins and Richard Fleming. Following their migration both women worked for a time on the Williams' family property where Te Aute College now stands.) Mary Mullins had also died young, at thirty-five, by which time she had given birth to eight children, six of whom also found their way to Aotearoa.

Kate left Ireland at twenty-one for the siren attractions of life on the Cape Road in coastal Taranaki; twenty-three when the splendidly named Father Claudius Celestine Cognet married her to a man seventeen years her senior (the wedding took place in Ōkato on 25 September 1898, but the reception was held in the one-room schoolhouse in Pungarehu, which had been the AC's blockhouse in 1881 and Te Whiti and Tohu's prison for a month following the November invasion); and seventy-seven when she died in New Plymouth on 24 February 1952.

Kate Fleming appears to have been an uncompromising character: she might be thought of as having been a difficult woman before that term became a badge of honour. In particular, her decision to keep hold of the three farms after Andrew's death rather than give them to Hugh, Andy and Tom (helpfully, Dick declared for the priesthood), who instead were required to work for wages, still sits poorly with some (including my mum).

Kate's position may have been unpopular, but it did mean she could provide for herself and her two 'spinster' daughters — and, much later, for Dick, who spent his final years living with his mother and sisters in the large, gloomy house on New Plymouth's Belt Road into which Kate moved six years before her death. (In a nice little twist, the house sported a front verandah grandly described as a 'piazza' on old building plans I came across. Dick, who would have sat in his fair share of these while in Rome, would have felt right at home.)

In any event, the received wisdom may be awry in several respects. One of the farms, of course, was hers and not her husband's. Another belonged (even if notionally) to Māori, and she could not have sold it even if she had wanted to. Furthermore, the contents of Andrew's final will, signed on 4 October 1909, cast the inherited story in a different light.[1] It is true that she is to get all of her husband's 'furniture and household effects', which he is willing to give to his 'dear wife Kate Gilhooly absolutely'. But he is absolutely not willing to give her ownership of any land.

Instead, Andrew leaves all his 'real and personal estate unto my Trustees', who are to 'allow my said wife to carry on my farming business and to take the net profits thereof for her own benefit so long during her widowhood as she shall desire'. (But conditions apply, as we shall see.) Moreover, the trustees are given 'absolute discretion' to make decisions regarding investment in the land and, although this can occur only with Kate's consent, to let or sell parts or all of the farm. Kate is to be provided for, but she does not get ownership of Andrew's land when he dies. A little bizarrely, however, she does get 'use [of] all my live and dead agricultural stock and implements'.

(As I was writing this section it occurred to me that Kate's purchase of her own farm was looking increasingly

Two contrasting photos of Kate Gilhooly (or Gran Gilhooly, as she is still referred to by my mother's generation). In one she is holding my grandfather Hugh, her first child, who was born in 1898, the year in which Kate Fleming married the much older Andrew Gilhooly. The second was probably taken after she had moved to New Plymouth from the Coast, and was living at Belt Road with her daughters Moll and Liz, and with a very ill Dick Gilhooly. She strikes me as someone you wouldn't mess with.

like a smart move on her part. Then I recalled the provenance of Section 102 and regretted the flippant thought I'd just had. But that thought, crass though it may be, came to me perfectly naturally — and that is important because it reveals just how deeply ingrained the forgetting has become.)

As to the conditions that attach: the first is that Kate 'shall suitably maintain and educate my infant children under the age of twenty one years' and 'give a home to such of my daughters as shall be unmarried'. (Neither Moll nor Liz will marry; both are living with Kate when she dies.) The second is that each year Kate shall hand over three-quarters of the farms' profits to the trustees 'for the maintenance, education and benefit of my children in equal shares', the remaining quarter being for 'her personal use and benefit'.

So it seems to me that the story of Kate's obduracy is not quite correct, even if it is consistent with a tendency to try to put 'difficult women' in their place. On the death of her husband there were only two farms in play, not three, and neither became hers to sell: Andrew placed control of both in the hands of his trustees.[2] Neither does she recoup the profits from Section 44 or the farm on the Opourapa Road: most of them go to her children. Yet all these years later Kate continues to cop a bit of flak for having chosen not to hand over control of the farms to her sons.

Vocation

None of which would have much bothered Richard Thomas Gilhooly on 19 October 1910, on which day he became the fourth child and third son of Kate and Andrew. In total, and in time, as well as Dick there were Hugh (my maternal grandfather), Andy, Mary (only ever known as Moll, the one whose duty in life it will eventually be to look after an ageing mother, a dying brother and a sick sister, in that order) and Tom and Liz, the twins.

There is no record of Dick's early years, but there are glimpses of the world in which he grew up on the Coast. They come from newspaper reports of the time, most of which concern his uncles.

Of the women few traces can be found. There is a reference to a meeting of the Cape Egmont Dairy Company in 1932, following which afternoon tea was served by 'Mesdames', among whom were Dick's mother Kate and his oldest sister Moll. (Mesdames were duly accorded a vote of thanks.) Kate is also mentioned fleetingly in the obituary of her youngest brother, Patrick Fleming ('Coastal Pioneer', rings out the *Opunake Times* on 11 October 1949), whose funeral Dick conducted at St Joseph's in New Plymouth.

The one Gilhooly woman who does have a reasonable media profile — largely because of her musical talents, which were put to good use up and down the Coast (and, from time to time, further afield) — is Dick's younger sister Liz. In 1933 she plays the piano at the annual concert of the Pungarehu school where, once the kids were done, the floor was promptly cleared for dancing. Four years later she is at the dance concluding the 'Her Majesty the Baby Carnival', which raised money for the Rāhotu Plunket room. (For the record, in the fundraising stakes Baby Green from Rāhotu edged out Baby Fleming from Pungarehu and Baby Chapman from the Wārea and Newall Road area.)

The same year there is also a 'monster dance' at the Rāhotu hall for the local 'cheese-punchers' (at which her twin brother Tom won the Gay Gordons competition). And on occasion she and Dick provided a brother–sister act at weddings, Dick officiating over the nuptials and Liz providing the music. (In 1935 the bride, a cousin from Hastings, wore an 'Anne Boleyn collar', which I am assured by my daughters is an actual thing but which nonetheless sounds slightly concerning.)[1]

Liz, though, is an exception. It is another matter as far as the Gilhooly men are concerned. Of them there are many traces. Dick's oldest brother, Hugh, who first farmed Kate's land and then shifted across the South Road to Section 44, was chair of the Taranaki Rugby Football Union between 1949 and 1958 and, later, made a life member of the union (as was his brother Tom, who bought Kate's farm after her death). Between 1929 and 1945 Hugh was also president of the Rāhotu club, whom he represented on the Taranaki Union's management committee from 1937 until 1959.

(Following his death his family presented the Hugh Gilhooly Memorial Cup to the club, which for years was on the line each time Rāhotu played Ōpunake. In 1995 the Rāhotu, Ōpunake and Ōkato clubs merged to form the Coastal Rugby Club — reverting to the same name that appears on the 1881 photo I have of Hugh's father standing with his AC Coastal rugby teammates. The cup itself appears to be lost.)

In a publication celebrating a century of Taranaki rugby, Peter Burke, who coached the All Blacks during the 1981 Springbok tour, recalls that Hugh 'beat the Southland drinking champ down at the Bluff at the annual provincial rugby drinking competition. Hughie won by a mile with Southland three glasses still on the bar when he finished.'[2] On another occasion members of a Taranaki Rugby Football Union subcommittee debating the weighty question of club boundaries resolved the issue in Hugh's vegetable garden 'sometime in the dark hours after midnight'.

It seems that Hugh, like his father Andrew in his early days, was not much for farming. My mother's view is that, rather than tend to the farm, he preferred to attend meetings. Of these there was no shortage, for in addition to those of various rugby organisations he also went to meetings of the Pungarehu school committee (which he sat on for twenty-one years, eighteen of them as chair), the Taranaki Hospital Board, the Cape Egmont Dog Trials Club (of which he was the inaugural president), the Loyal Rahotu Lodge (in which he attained the rank of District Grand Master in 1941), the Cape Egmont Dairy Company and the Egmont County Council and its myriad subcommittees.

When not at meetings he was inclined to ride his bike into New Plymouth and back again with his brother Tom to watch the Friday night boxing — a round trip of roughly 50 kilometres along gravel roads. (Former governor-general Bernard Freyberg, who feared that with 'mechanization, buses and cinemas, if we are not careful, we shall not be the hardy race we were', would have been proud of Hughie and Tom.)[3]

On these occasions the milking would fall to Mum's brother, who was always known as Tui, and her mother Millie, who also cooked for a family of eleven when all nine children and her husband were home. Mum can't recall her father ever reciprocating and doing a bit of cooking or housework (my father did both, which may explain why his mother-in-law liked him so much and his father-in-law was initially suspicious). Hugh may not have been an enthusiastic farmer, but he could dance: in 1919 he and a Miss M. Gibson won the waltzing competition during a night out at the Pungarehu Town Hall.[4]

Dick's older brother Andy was, if anything, an even bigger fan of meetings. Andy farmed on the Opourapa Road property for thirty-six years and his obituary — he died on

28 February 1963 — makes for impressive reading. At various times in his life Andy was a member of nine community bodies: the New Plymouth Cycling and Athletic League, the Coastal Boxing Association, the Rahotu Hall Committee, the Rahotu Athletic Club, the Rahotu Manchester Unity of the Order of Oddfellows, Federated Farmers, the Young Farmers' Club, the St Pius X Catholic Church Committee and the Taranaki Centre of the New Zealand Athletic, Cycling and Axemen's Union. One, perhaps two at most of those organisations survive. The rest were part of a provincial New Zealand laced together by dense networks of associations, clubs, fairs, churches and dairy factories that has long since slipped away.

Dick himself only starts to come into focus when he sails from the Coast to Auckland and enrols as a boarding pupil at Sacred Heart College in February 1922.[5] From the start his academic work stands out. In his first year — during which his father dies — he receives the highest mark in the Royal Academy Examinations. The next year he picks up prizes for third in Latin and fourth in science. He is bested in both by a boy called Bradanovich, whose name is often in the school's various roll calls of success over the next several years, usually one or two places ahead of Dick's. Nineteen twenty-two is the beginning of an era of Bradanovichian dominance that Dick is to end spectacularly in his final year at school.

Boxing features prominently during his time in Auckland. There is this from the school magazine of 1922: 'When the warm summer days grew shorter, and the winter months drew near, boxing became perhaps our most popular pastime.' You expect to read about long, earnest conversations around a campfire or some such — but instead you get pugilism. On 20 September Dick and a similarly slight lad called Quinn fought 'two very strenuous rounds' in the Midget weight division (the demesne of those weighing less than seven stone, or 44 kilograms), in what the magazine's editor hailed as 'undoubtedly the best bout of the evening'.

That fight ends in a tie, but later the same evening Dick wins a second bout and then a third. This takes him into the final against O'Regan — which he duly loses. Dick may be small but he has stamina. He is going to need it.

Two months later he is on a different kind of stage in the role of Célestine, a chef, in the French Dialogue at the school's annual concert at St Benedict's Hall. Five items later he's back on, playing the role of Feeble in the recruiting scene from Shakespeare's *Henry IV Part II.* Feeble has a total of seven lines, all of them fairly short (as in: 'Here sir'), so I imagine Dick concentrated on Célestine, which was an altogether more substantial role.

Towards the end of 1924, in his third year at Sacred Heart, a sequence of letters is exchanged that set the course for the remainder of Dick's life.[6] Since his arrival at Sacred Heart Dick had been a member of the Sodality of the Blessed Virgin Mary. The society was directed by Brother Borgia, who — and perhaps this had something to do with the death of his father when he was only thirteen — was to become a significant figure in Dick's life. That process began with a letter Borgia wrote in early October to the coadjutor archbishop of Wellington, Thomas O'Shea.[7]

Coadjutor archbishop is an impressive title. The role of the coadjutor is to assist the diocesan archbishop. It's a sort of proxy role, insofar as on the death, retirement, resignation or reassignation of the latter the former takes office. O'Shea was a religious and political heavyweight in the Catholic Church. He was born in 1870 in San Francisco and served as coadjutor to Archbishop Francis Redwood (the first New Zealander to study for the priesthood overseas) from 1913 until Redwood's death in January 1935, at which point he in turn became archbishop.

(For an awful lot of Catholic school students, however, O'Shea is important for a rather different reason. The O'Shea Shield is an annual competition between Catholic secondary schools in the Wellington and Palmerston North dioceses and is a Very Big Deal indeed. It consists of several days of fiercely contested encounters — drama, debating, scripture reading, the answering of religious questions, that sort of thing — that for generations of us was the undisputed heavyweight highlight of the school year. I swam for my school and played in the First XV but the O'Shea Shield was bigger than both. With my friends Bernard Leuthart and Patrick Bennett I competed in it with great gusto and no success whatsoever as a student at Francis Douglas College in the late 1970s.

Winning something — anything — would have been nice, but it wasn't really the point. The point was the opportunity to spend time in the company of Catholic girls. I didn't win anything there, either, but was incapable of learning from serial failure and approached each new O'Shea Shield season with hopeless renewed optimism.)

Borgia's 1924 letter draws the archbishop's attention to a 'boarder here at the College who has made up his mind to be a priest, and who has every mark of a true vocation'. (Which rather suggests that had my great-uncle been able to compete in the shield — he wasn't, because it was first contested in 1946 — he would have been insufferably successful.) Gratifyingly for Dick's descendants, Borgia goes on to note that the boarder in question 'belongs to an excellent family and is an excellent boy himself in every way'. Even at this early point, judging from Borgia's further observations, Dick seems to have decided on becoming a secular priest — one who lives and works in the world at large, instead of joining a particular religious order.

In his response O'Shea expresses 'no hesitation in accepting [Dick] as a student for the priesthood, and will sanction his entrance into the Seminary at Mosgiel as soon as he is ready, or when he has passed the Matriculation examination'.[8] Had things proceeded as planned, Dick would have entered the seminary at the age of fourteen. (At that age I was beginning my fourth form, planning a winning strategy for that year's O'Shea Shield and trying to figure out how to get a young woman from New Plymouth Girls' High School to go to a movie with me. *Piranha* was playing, as I recall.) That this is a little precocious is not lost on Brother Borgia, who underscores the word 'fourteen' when alerting O'Shea to Dick's age. As it happens, things did not work out as Dick may have hoped, but all the same the die was being cast.

The next letter is a brief one from Dick himself to the rector of Holy Cross Seminary, Father Morkane, sent in early November 1924, in which he seeks permission to enter the seminary.[9] Reinforcing Borgia's earlier reference, he points to 'a desire since I was young' to become a secular priest in the archdiocese of Wellington.[10] But this is followed by a second letter to Morkane four weeks later, in which Dick explains that on Borgia's advice his mother has decided that rather than enter the seminary in 1925 he should remain at school for one more year.[11]

It looks as if during the month separating the two letters a significant conversation took place between Kate Gilhooly and Brother Borgia. Perhaps Borgia had had second thoughts about Dick's age. If so, then he must have managed to bring Kate around to his thinking because in his initial approach to O'Shea, Borgia had made it clear that Kate was 'anxious that he enter Mosgiel next year' (i.e., in 1925). Whatever the case, in the event reason prevails:

fourteen does seem inordinately young to enter a seminary. Matters are put on hold, and so there is the matter of Dick's sixth form to attend to.

Dick works up a serious head of academic steam in his final year at Sacred Heart. He gains a Higher Leaving Certificate, is awarded a Senior National Scholarship to university (for which he ranks third in the country), takes out the Coulahan Gold Medal for Good Conduct, and receives — in a sign from above, surely — the Gold Medal for Religious Knowledge. He is still boxing, a little heavier now and the champion of the 8st 4lb class, and is also one of five editors of the school's annual magazine. Inevitably, Bradanovich also has an excellent year in 1925, captaining both the First XV and the First XI, holding down a librarian's position and commanding No. 3 Platoon of the Cadet Corps.

And where Dick's performances in the Junior Debating Society are damned with faint praise ('impresse[s] very favourably' on the 'few occasions on which he has spoken'), I read that Bradanovich has a 'superabundance of confidence, and always advance[s] his theories, sound in the main, with plenty of determination'. But then there is this: 'However, [Bradanovich] at times remind[s] us of that Shakespearean character who "talks a great deal of nothing".' And I confess to feeling a little ashamed at revelling in the fact that in his final year Dick is the top

Above: The editors of the 1925 edition of the Sacred Heart College magazine: Dick is on the right and Bradanovich the left. SACRED HEART COLLEGE ARCHIVES

Below: Dick, shortly after his ordination in 1933. PUKE ARIKI

overall student in Form VI.B, ending Bradanovich's reign and relegating him to third place.

Dick also writes an essay on the Great Liberator, Daniel O'Connell — who secured political emancipation for Ireland's Catholics in 1829 — for the McVeagh Memorial Prize Essay. His effort is dismissed rather sniffily as 'effective', although it is still good enough to win third place. Bradanovich doesn't even make the podium. But here is another indication that Dick knew exactly where he wanted to go, because O'Connell had a close relationship with the Pontifical Irish College, where Dick will find himself a student in a little under five years. (So close, in fact, that O'Connell bequeathed his heart to the college, which somehow or other managed to lose it.)

As with the dense social networks of people living on the Coast, the world of Dick's secondary schooling is also long gone. The profusion of academic awards, scholarships and miscellaneous other prizes on offer in those days is striking. The year my great-uncle took out a Senior National Scholarship, various of his classmates secured Junior University Scholarships, University National Scholarships, University Entrance Scholarships, Higher Leaving Certificates, Matriculation (full or partial), Senior National Scholarships, Public Service Entrance, Intermediate and Proficiency Certificates and something called Solicitors' General Knowledge. All that and the possibility of boxing, firing a rifle and playing a French chef in the same year.

There is one final letter from 1925.[12] Almost exactly a

year on from his last approach to the rector of Holy Cross, Dick again writes to Morkane requesting entrance into the seminary for the 1926 year (and asking, touchingly, what 'outfit' is required). Permission is granted. When the man after whom I am named enters the seminary he will be just fifteen. A year older than fourteen, sure, but it still feels extraordinarily young to me. At the same age I was still stubbornly failing on all counts at the O'Shea Shield.

Over the next four years Dick prepares for life as a priest by studying philosophy (1926/27) and theology (1928/29) at the Holy Cross Seminary in Mosgiel. What little I know of his time there continues to come from Sacred Heart's yearbook (which, remarkably, goes on providing periodic reports of Dick, Bradanovich and other old boys until Dick's death some thirty years after he left the school). From the yearbook I learn that in his first year in Dunedin Dick adds handball and tennis to his sporting repertoire.

In his second he joins the seminary's choir and is an active participant in amateur theatricals: no longer Feeble, he of the seven lines of dialogue, but landing the lead role in a musical comedy situated in ancient Rome. The mention of singing is important, for following his own Roman adventure Dick developed a reputation for having a beautiful tenor voice.

However, once he begins his academic exploration of theology in 1928 all mention of sporting and cultural frippery vanishes, possibly because by the end of his final year his old school's yearbook confidently pronounces him 'an able exponent of the Thomistic Doctrines', mastery of which would not have left much time for hitting small balls or gallivanting around stages.

At the end of November of that year in Mosgiel, Archbishop O'Shea writes to Father Morkane agreeing that Dick would make a suitable candidate for overseas study. Morkane has made the first move, but O'Shea indicates that he was already of the view that Dick should leave for such purposes. More than that, he is also of a mind to send Dick not only to Europe but also to America, as 'he must [be] the kind of student that will profit to the utmost by such a chance'.

An insight into O'Shea's enthusiastic support for Dick lies in a letter written in 1930 by Dunedin-based James Kelly, then the editor of the *New Zealand Tablet*, to the rector of the Pontifical Irish College, John Hagan.[13] Hagan, a Dubliner, was vice-rector (1904–20) and then rector (1920–30) of the college and an important player in both Irish nationalist and Church politics. Hagan and Kelly (whose uncle was archbishop of Sydney and a former rector of the Irish College) became friends when they were students together at the college in the late 1890s.

Hagan would go on to become rector while Kelly, having developed a close relationship with the demon drink and a penchant for unsuitable company, would move out to New Zealand in 1913 to reboot his career, editing the *Tablet* between 1917 and 1931, and thereby joining the sprawling network of Irish- and Roman-educated Catholic priests who edited newspapers at home or abroad.[14]

The friendship would stand Kelly in good stead when Hagan, who did a great deal to assist Australian and New Zealand clergy navigate the politics of Irish nationalism, intervened to stop him being removed as editor in the face of Rome's anger at his use of the *Tablet* to advocate Irish nationalism. Neither did Kelly's anti-imperialism stance against conscription and description of Queen Victoria as 'a certain fat old German woman' in a 1917 edition of the *Tablet* greatly endear him to New Zealand's secular powers, who briefly threatened to charge him with sedition and to shut the publication down.[15]

In the end, having alienated both religious and lay authorities — as well as a fair few of his own colleagues (Kelly was seemingly an 'indefatigable gossip' who once described Auckland's Catholic clergy as 'a gang of [God's] sycophants')[16] — he resigned as editor of the periodical and returned to priestly duties. Kelly spent his last years as parish priest in Dick's home town of Pungarehu and died in 1939.

His funeral service was held in St Martin de Tours, the small church in Pungarehu established by the French Marist who married Dick's parents, and in which my own mum and dad were also wed, and his grave in the Ōkato cemetery is about 3 metres away from those of Andrew and Kate Gilhooly.

But in 1930 Kelly's letter to Hagan explains that O'Shea has had a 'dreadful run of duds and refuses to have any more Irish priests'. Time to nurture the home-grown talent instead, to which end O'Shea asks Morkane to get Dick to visit him in Wellington on his way home to Pungarehu from Mosgiel to 'see what can be done'. Theologically, politically, culturally, academically and historically: Dick is about to venture into the heart of Roman Catholicism.

Are we there yet?

The Church authorities decide that Dick will be in Rome by October, in time to begin the 1930–31 academic year. He is to be based at the Pontifical Irish College and study at the Pontifical Lateran University. Until the boat sails he is to knock around in Mosgiel. In March of that interregnum Morkane receives a letter from a Father McRae. McRae is based at the Chancery Office attached to the Archbishop's House at 7 Paterson Street, near the Basin Reserve in Wellington (it had been built in 1869 for the well-known Wellington business person and member of Parliament William Waring Taylor), and explains that the archbishop has put things in train by approaching the Irish College endorsing Dick's candidacy as a student.[1] He reassures the rector of Holy Cross that 'we don't anticipate any difficulty in making a satisfactory arrangement'.

As with Brother Borgia, and perhaps for similar reasons, the Right Reverend Dr Father Arthur J. McRae is to become a significant figure in Dick's life. While Dick is in Rome McRae is his primary point of contact in the Catholic Church in New Zealand: the person who arranges payment of his living costs, organises the paperwork for his ordination as a subdeacon, and generally keeps young Gilhooly up to date with goings-on back home.

McRae was intellectually and politically impressive. Ordained in 1921, he had gained a PhD at the Catholic University in Washington DC during the mid-1920s and worked as chancellor at St Joseph's presbytery on Paterson Street in Mount Victoria, Wellington, until his death in 1964.[2] He was also a physically imposing man, clocking in at just under 2.3 metres (or 7 feet).

The Turnbull Library holds a photo of him standing alongside five other priests outside the bishop's palace in Dunedin in 1948: he towers over his contemporaries and has the look of a man you really should not cross. Members of McRae's former parish of Kilbirnie recall nervous mothers watching him holding their babies in one huge palm as he baptised them.[3]

From that point until his death Dick was to benefit greatly from McRae's support. In his missive to Morkane, McRae admits that 'it was a great relief to me to learn that there is prospect of raising most of the money necessary among Dick's own relatives'. In 1930 money was a concern for a great many people. It certainly preoccupied Dick. In his first correspondence with McRae, also penned in mid-March 1930, he confirms that he has set about assessing the costs of the trip to Rome and discussing these with 'my people'. He estimates that a second-class berth on a boat from Australia to Rome will cost £102.

Life in Rome itself will amount to around £100 per annum, including the two occasions during the four-year course during which 'colonial students may travel' and possibly also the costs associated with the use of the 'villa in the hills' that the college's students have access to. (In fact there were two villas to which the seminarians repaired from time to time, in Formia and Tivoli, neither of which the college now owns. During the Second World War, after Dick's time, the Wehrmacht used the Tivoli property as a command post, and the caves underneath the building 'were used for a much more sinister purpose'.)[4]

The discussions Dick has with 'his people' about covering these expenses considered two options — 'funding models', we would probably call them today — both of which he had previously canvassed with McRae while in Wellington late in 1929. The first calls for 'something of the nature of a presentation [to] be arranged on the occasion of my departure to help defray expenses', and the second 'that four or five of my more comfortable relatives be approached to contribute £20 to my expenses'.

The idea of a whip-round is initially given short shrift, Dick informing McRae that

> Mother and the whole family discussed the letter [presumably one from Dick setting out the choices] and contents, and claiming their natural right to education of their own, declared they could not approve of the first plan, but were not averse to the second. They said they would club together, my married brothers as well

> assisting, and contribute £100 a year. They did not mind if my relatives were to present a sum of money on the occasion of my departure, but that they [the relatives] should enter into any sort of contract to pay £20 per year each, was to them [the immediate family] repulsive.[5]

But while the family is willing to chip in, the establishment is not let off the hook entirely, because Dick politely asks McRae to establish if Archbishop O'Shea is in a position to meet the pension for the Irish College of £50 a year. What is proposed is a sort of dollar-for-dollar approach: Dick's people will find £50 a year for the five years he will need to be in Rome, with the Church meeting the rest of his living costs. A month later, Dick receives a response in which McRae expresses his appreciation for the commitment Dick's family is making, and gives an undertaking that the archdiocese will meet the balance through 'lay contributions to the Seminary Collection'.

There is a slight risk with outsourcing Dick's costs in this way, we are told, because the collection has a habit of falling short of the required levels, but McRae assures Dick 'there are still possible resources that I have not yet tapped'. And so the secular and sacred economies join forces in a mutually beneficial arrangement: the Gilhooly family gets the social status associated with providing a highly educated priest for mother Church while O'Shea gets to end his 'dreadful run of duds'.

O'Shea hears back from Michael Curran, the new rector

of the Pontifical Irish College, at the end of March.[6] For both the archbishop and the novice the news is good: a place for Dick at the college is confirmed, and Curran takes it that Dick will 'enter for a rank in 3rd theology' at the Pontifical Lateran University, which the students of Irish College generally attend, commencing in October.[7] Curran also warns that the Lateran has become more exacting in its admission requirements, such that 'it is essential that [Dick] bring a certificate stating that he has completed one, two or three years theology, mentioning the subjects, and that he has passed his college examinations'.

A process of academic reform is under way and 'it is certain that the course for D.D. [doctorate of divinity] is to be extended to five years'. But the rector notes that 'as Mr Gilhooly is so underage that will be no hardship for him'.

And in the end there is, of course, a whip-round. This is the Coast, after all, and the opportunity for a full-blown shindig to mark the departure of a member of the community — especially one whose achievements have brought, and are about to bring, credit to that small corner of the world — was never going to be passed up.

The 24 September 1930 edition of the *New Zealand Tablet* dedicated a full page to Dick's farewell to the people of the Coast. The do comprised a 'gathering of 600 or 700, representatives of the whole coastal district, all sections of the community having gathered', who came together at the

Pungarehu Town Hall just before Dick left for an evening of music, dancing, cards, food and speeches. (Mostly in that order, although there appears to have been some competition between the 'nearly one hundred couples who were playing euchre in the supper hall' while Dick's sister, Liz, and other musicians were keeping the dancers going.)

Mr R. W. Fleming introduces Dick as a member of 'a well known and esteemed family'. (Richie Bill Fleming is not to be confused with Richie Mick Fleming, although my father never got them sorted — neither did he, an outsider and a townie to boot, ever fully get to grips with the thicket of Jims, Toms, Micks, Williams, Dicks and Hughs in my mother's family. Irish convention at the time was to name a first son after his paternal grandfather, the second after his maternal grandfather and the third after his father. Inevitably, certain names wound up on high rotation, and so you can see why Dad struggled to navigate his way through the complex system of Dick Jims, Willie Dicks, Richie Dicks and Dick Jacks, the last of whom — and this must have really finished poor Dad off — was also known as Dick Manihi.)

Father Kennedy, the parish priest at Ōpunake, notes approvingly that 'when many of his college mates were preparing to follow worldly professions, [Dick's] ideals and thoughts were raised to a higher and nobler plain'. (Yes, Bradanovich, that probably does mean you.) He then presents Dick with a birthday cake, a fountain pen and — at the end of the evening — 'a well-filled wallet of notes'.

Days later, Dick Gilhooly sails for Rome.

Via dei Ss Quattro

There follows a gap of nearly nine months before the letters from Rome start flowing. A great deal had to have happened in the interim, but there is no surviving record of Dick's trip across the oceans to Rome, his initial impressions of the Eternal City or his first encounters with the Pontifical Irish College on the Via dei Ss Quattro, just a short uphill stroll from the Colosseum. It must have been a time of tumult and excitement for him, but it remains frustratingly out of reach.

The archives of the Pontifical Irish College do hold one glimpse of his arrival. Dick registered with the college on 25 October 1930, a week after his twentieth birthday. The Latinisation of proper nouns in the formal records produces some charming results: Dick morphs into 'Ricardus', Andrew and Kate become the altogether more exotic 'Andreas' and 'Catharina', and Auckland is magically transformed into the Roman city 'Aucopolitan'. Imagine the howls of laughter those beautiful little twists would have occasioned in Pungarehu and Rāhotu.

Many of the buildings and streets where Ricardus was

to spend the next three years remain much as they were nearly a century ago. The Collegio Irlandese is still to be found in the elegant building tucked in behind stone walls at 1 Via dei Ss Quattro, the college's fifth location and the one to which it relocated from the church of Sant'Agata dei Goti in 1926 (thereby carving nearly half an hour off Dick's walk to the Lateran University).

The pontifical colleges — the oldest of which, the Almo Collegio Capranica, dates from 1417 — are where the 'officer corps' of the Roman Catholic workforce is trained.[1] Dick's place, the Irish College in Rome, was established in 1628. It is a fascinating institution, one of a number of Irish centres of higher learning scattered across Catholic Europe — others are in Salamanca, Louvain and Paris. Quite apart from their religious functions, those places helped keep Irish literature, art, scholarship and language alive across the centuries during which the English suppressed Catholicism in Ireland.

They have also helped shape both Irish and Catholic politics (and these did and do not necessarily pull in the same direction) around the world.[2] In the nineteenth and twentieth centuries, in particular, the Irish College was central to the process of 'Irish episcopal imperialism' that 'hibernicised' the hierarchies of the Catholic Church right around the English-speaking world, including in Aotearoa.[3]

As you might expect, then, the place is saturated with stories. Some are at the lower end of the spectrum of significance. There are anecdotes, for instance, proposing that the Irish College was established to keep Irish clerics away from those of other nations, for not only were they 'bad mixers' but they were known also for their insubordination and for drawing knives on other students from time to time (in particular Maronites and Englishmen, but sometimes on their own kind too).[4]

Other tales are central to any retelling of the story of the Irish diaspora. The best of these concerns the heart of Daniel O'Connell, the Great Liberator of Catholic Emancipation in Ireland and Great Britain (and the subject of Dick's school essay). O'Connell is said to have bequeathed his soul to God, his body to Ireland and his heart to Rome. The bequest duly outraged any number of Irish, who failed to see why Rome should get the good bit. Unhelpfully, O'Connell then died in Genoa in 1847, rather complicating the execution of the second and third of his bequests.

In any event, the heart eventually found its way to the college, where it received an elaborate funeral — only to be misplaced at some later point.[5] True, 1 Via dei Ss Quattro does have a very large, very marble vault which allegedly holds the heart in question, but the smart money is on the likelihood that the organ remains under a slab in the floor of the church of Sant'Agata dei Goti, where it was originally interred.

In November 1930 Dick composes the first of the six letters he will send to McRae from Rome.[6] Its primary and disappointingly prosaic purpose is to pass on to the archdiocese the bill for the coming year's pension. I want to hear about Rome, but Dick wants to sort out the practicalities. There are, thankfully, one or two insights into his new life. He reflects that he has 'grown more accustomed to the methods of the professors at Lateran University' (as an academic I can spot this kind of polite code a mile off), and that although the standard is 'very high, and the amount of work to be done very extensive, and rather difficult to cope with' — which is as close to a complaint as Ricardus Gilhooly ever gets in his Roman correspondence — he is 'now following most of [his] classes quite well'.

Those classes were being held at the Lateran, which was established by Pope Clement XIV in 1773 following the suppression of the Jesuits, and tasked with educating seminarians from the various pontifical colleges. Conveniently, by the time Dick arrived the main language of instruction was English, albeit an English 'spoken with a charming variety of accents'. Only one subject, Church history, was taught in Italian. Prayers back at the Irish College were another matter entirely: they are in Gaelic, which in Dick's view 'rivals Hebrew in difficulty'.

And he should know, explaining to McRae that 'Hebrew, incidentally, or my ignorance of Hebrew, is a slight handicap at the Lateran in scripture. I am still learning its alphabet.' The other students at the university are 'a very sociable crowd', and as to the discipline, it is 'very strict, but not unreasonable in its demands'.

It has been quite the year for Dick. In March he was mucking about in Mosgiel, but as he celebrated his first

Christmas abroad at the end of 1930 he was studying at a Roman university, learning Hebrew, Latin and Italian, and answering to the name of Ricardus. He is barely twenty and he is a long way from the Coast in all possible respects.

It is February 1931, and Dick has received an unsigned letter on blank paper. However, we know that it is from Father McRae because the writer apologises to Dick for the late payment of the bill for the pension.[7] (The money order, made out to the 'Collegium Hibernorium de Urbe' to the value of £44, arrives two days after the letter does.) The correspondence is memorable for two reasons. The first is McRae's decidedly un-priestly observation that '[b]y this [time] you will be a sort of cross between a full-blown Wop & a Gaelic speaking Celt'. I imagine that this is meant as a compliment to Dick's efforts at integrating himself into the life of the college, but the casual racism sticks in the craw these days.

The balance of the letter is given over to the Napier earthquake, which McRae describes as 'a small affair in comparison with the Italian average but still a severe experience for this little land'. He had accompanied Archbishop O'Shea to Napier the day after the quake, and acknowledged that they 'were not able to do anything, of course, except offer sympathy. Still the presence of the Abp. meant a good deal to the priests & sisters who had suffered in the ordeal.'

Dick pens a long, six-page response to McRae two months later.[8] This is one of the few times when he tells us a little about life at the Irish College. He bemoans his dismal lack of progress towards becoming 'a cross between a full-blown Wop and a Gaelic speaking Celt', which he attributes to the fact that 'we don't get much of an opportunity in this institution to express our feelings in the dago lingo'. (Clearly, casual racism is not the sole preserve of the senior clergy.) As to opportunities to speak in Gaelic, these are 'confined to the "Our Father", the "Hail Mary" and "Gloria" for chapel use'. And it 'requires no little effort to master that much in parrot fashion'. It is possible, and perhaps likely, that Dick's parents spoke or were at least on passing terms with Gaelic, but the language of his forebears is a foreign tongue to him now.

Then it is on to the imminent departure of Bill Flynn, following which Dick will be the 'sole N.Z. representative here'. There is also reference to 'a breakfast–dinner combination type of meal lasting some hours'. I suspect the Italians just called it lunch, but the experience of lingering over a long meal in the middle of the day is not one that Dick would have had much practice of on the farm on the South Road, at Sacred Heart College or in Mosgiel. And there's another thing. Dick mentions the ordination of Jim Fanning, from Perth, 'who is aged fifty-two, no less, but still has years of vitality in him'. Dick does not know that his own vitality will start to leach away within the year.

Plenty of time for that, though, for Dick is keen to

move on and explain the structure of his course to McRae. It looks like this. At the end of their first year of study theology students sit for a bachelor of divinity (BD), the exams for which cover the course work from that year. Two years later they have another series of exams for a licentiate of sacred theology (STL), which encompasses third-year theology and the previous two years' worth of course work. Finally, at the end of the four-year course, students sit the exams for and complete the thesis associated with a doctorate of divinity (DD), for which purposes all four years are examinable.

Rector Curran's suggested course of study for Dick would have him sitting for his DD in June 1934, coinciding nicely with the formal age at which priests could be ordained. But he got there by mid-1932, two years ahead of schedule — and in this letter to McRae we find out how that came about. In April 1931 Dick's 'regular examiner in the oral exams in the house', a Father Patten, had a few conversations with the college's vice-rector. Both men seem to have formed the view — prompted perhaps by the new regulations which were about to push the DD out a further year — that in Dick's case it would make sense to speed things up.

They proposed that he sit his BD exams at the end of the 1931 academic year (i.e., in June/July), as was the usual practice, but that he should then — following a 'holiday period' in which he would need to knuckle down and do some serious academic work — sit the STL exams in November of that *same* year. (In the event he did so in

October.) Effectively, the plan was to examine Dick on three years' worth of work at the end of this first year of study. And that, if successful, would allow him to sit his DD at the end of the 1932 academic year — crunching a four-year course of study down into two.

That is quite some process of acceleration. I am not sure Brother Borgia would have approved, and wonder whether the pressure this put Dick under contributed to what was to come. Dick himself admits to McRae that the proposal is ambitious, but is quietly bullish about his prospects all the same ('Now, I really do think I have quite a fair chance of succeeding in this programme'). Foolishly, he goes on to tempt fate, saying that 'the health bug has not troubled me in the least since coming here, and I don't think it is likely to interfere in this little business'.

What interests me is the inference that a 'health bug' might have troubled him in the past. Not since arriving in Rome, perhaps, but by implication at some prior point. Perhaps it was not Rome that was to kill Dick after all, which is the family story that has been passed down. Perhaps the Eternal City was just the final way station on a journey that began in Mosgiel. Or Auckland. Or the Coast.

In his next letter, Dick tells his mentor that he has been informed by the rector he is to take his '[Roman] Vicariate exam for subdiaconate late in June or early in July'.[9] Until the office was abolished by Pope Paul VI in the mid-1970s, a subdeaconate was the order that was taken — along with a vow of celibacy — prior to becoming a deacon and, subsequently, a priest. To that end Dick mentions that he has applied for dimissorials for all three major orders (subdeacon, deacon and priest). A dimissorial is a letter from an ecclesiastical superior to a subject. In this case, it is a way through which Archbishop O'Shea frees Dick from his (O'Shea's) jurisdiction — so perhaps Dick saw some possibility that he might, *contra* his earlier protestations, be ordained outside of the archdiocese of Wellington.

Having got the formal business out of the way, Dick reveals a little of what is going on for him. The tone is characteristically stoic and understated. 'Hot weather,' he tells us, 'much mental exertion and multitudes of flies have made the last few weeks a little trying.' The mental exertion can be attributed to the study he is undertaking for his BD exams. 'Feeling in good trim,' he says, but then immediately guards against hubris by admitting to McRae that 'whilst quietly confident and all that sort of thing, I have not as yet commenced to sign my name B.D. If I can knock out a decent mark it will be a tonic for the summer gallop towards S.T.L. Of course, the fact that it is hard to gallop in hot weather will no doubt act as a brake on my impetuosity.'

There is also — and this is rare in Dick's letters, as befits a young man with a spiritual vocation — a nod to current events in the secular domain. 'I notice postage on letters from N.Z. up these days,' he writes, adding that he has also 'heard of the 10% reduction Bill. I hope the country's finance remains safe.' In fact, at the time the nation's finances were looking none too good, for an 'economic blizzard . . . had long since commenced its devastating influence on New Zealand industry and finance': export prices were falling, legislation had reduced the salaries of public servants by 10 per cent, and the Arbitration Court had decreed a 10 per cent reduction in wages.[10]

But the hot weather, mental exertion and flies do not stand a chance, and 'Ricardus Gilhooly (III Theol)' duly completes his baccalaureate in July 1931, with a mark of 21/30, in the disciplines of *Theologiae Fundamentalis* and *Historiae Ecclesiasticae*.[11] Three months later — four weeks ahead of schedule — he also obtains his licentiate with 36/60, adding *Iuris Canonici* and *Liturgiae Sacrae* to his programme.

The examination record also contains the college rector's succinct assessments of Dick's standard of discipline (which barely passes muster as 'satisfactory', leaving me to wonder why it wasn't better), his Spoken Eloquence ('good'), Spoken Ceremonie ('good') and Gregorian Chant (which, unsurprisingly given his reputation as a fine voice, was assessed as 'very good'). Rector Curran concludes that 'Mr Gilhooly has given complete satisfaction during this his first year in this college. Being very young (born 10.IX.1910) he can only be presented for subdeaconship this year . . . His health has been good.' And there it is again — a passing, perfunctory reference to health.

Dick's third letter to McRae that year, a four-pager sent in early November, begins with a slightly abashed request-cum-apology.[12] Having thanked McRae for the latter's rapid work on ensuring the necessary papers (the dimissorials) were despatched to Rome, Dick finds 'it necessary — like Oliver Twist — to come back for more'. As all good bureaucracies are prone to do from time to time, Roman officialdom has changed the rules regarding the correct application form for the dimissorials, necessitating the completion of a whole new set of papers. McRae will be inconvenienced, but the delay will not greatly affect Dick, because ordinations are common in Rome, occurring 'here every couple of months, and at X-mas, Easter and June every week, so I shall have ample opportunity to receive the order'.

Dick also makes it clear that his exam success was not a foregone conclusion. To achieve a degree a student needs to gain a 60 per cent passing grade (not for the Lateran anything so mundane as a 50 per cent pass), and while he managed an average of 70 per cent for his BD exams in July, for the STL Dick counts himself 'rather lucky. I just scraped home with the necessary 60% average.'

Dick accounts for this close-run thing by explaining that he 'had the work really well done' heading into the exams, but then came 'a most distressing session with the Sacraments Professor on a small point in Transubstantiation. He taught it to me in the examination hall. I must have received very little from him.' (How often, I wonder, has an encounter of that nature ever been described in a letter from Rome to Aotearoa?) But even though Dick has revised two full years' worth of work in the four months between his BD and STL exams, there is no sense of triumph or self-congratulation. Instead, 'Considering again that a very large number went down in this degree I count myself fortunate.'

And so attention turns to the coming academic year, at the end of which Dick will attempt his doctorate of divinity. The workload looks intimidating: 'the whole course [of four years] will be on, a thesis has to be written, and . . . there is no time to waste'. It is so onerous that Dick 'didn't budge outside the villas at Formia and Tivoli during the vacation, study detaining me'. He did go swimming every day, which made 'villa life agreeable'. It is the thesis that bothers Dick most, and he promises to keep McRae informed of progress on that front.

The rest of the letter is given over to bits and bobs of news. McRae is informed that the 'present financial stress' (a reference to the Great Depression) has forced the college to increase the pension from £44 to £50. Dick wryly notes that the latest batch of 'N.Z. and Mosgiel products' is settling into college life and 'enjoying at the present time the first thrills of the Roman class-room', and expresses disappointment that his workload will prevent him from attending 'the Congress'.[13]

The final artefact that survives from 1931 is an end-of-year report from Rector Curran to Archbishop O'Shea.[14] Dick has once again 'given full satisfaction' and Curran expects him to 'do better at his exams this year as he will be more practised in the use of Latin'. He also asks O'Shea this: 'In case [Dick] does succeed in getting his D.D. is it the intention of his superiors that he should take out the degree in Canon Law?' And he points out that even 'with the most liberal dispensation', Dick cannot be ordained until 1933.

Zenith

Nineteen thirty-two is the biggest year in Dick Gilhooly's life. It is both sublime and grotesque, a year in which he reaches the heights only to be diagnosed with a disease that will ruin his academic career, restrict his professional life and, slowly and painfully, kill him. It is the year of the DD, but also of TB.

It starts brightly enough, with a note from McRea in early January congratulating Dick on 'having managed matters so well up to this' and acknowledging that his success comes as little surprise in Wellington, because '[o]f course it's only what we expected. That's the worst of having a reputation. People tend to take things for granted.'

McRae's attention then turns to what the future might hold for Dick. While there is 'nothing very definite in the Archbishop's mind' at that point, McRae himself is 'still of the opinion that a course in the Education Deptmt. at C.U.A. is the best proposition both for us and for yourself'. McRae is writing from the Rehabilitation School of the Catholic University of America in Washington DC. Had things taken a different course Dick might have headed from the Old

World to the New. But he also concedes that 'England might have much to offer in this connection', and accepts that given his 'additional experience & the new contacts' he will have made in Rome, Dick will have views of his own. McRae actively solicits them: 'The Archbishop (unfortunately I feel) depends a good deal upon me for a lead in affairs such as these and I would like to keep everything in sight — the needs of the Archdiocese, your inclinations etc.'[1]

McRae is not the only one thinking of Dick's future. O'Shea, too, has Dick on his mind when he writes to Monsignor Curran early in 1932, ostensibly to thank him for the report on Dick's progress.[2] But the critical paragraph is the second one, in which O'Shea expresses both a 'wish that [Dick] should take his degree in Canon Law' and the view that 'it would be no use for him to leave Rome until he is ordained priest'.

The doctorate, it is becoming clear, is just the first phase of the project the Church has in mind for Dick: 'When he is finished with you he will still be a young man, [and] we intend to send him elsewhere to study other subjects and gain experience that will be useful for the work that will be given him on his return to New Zealand.' There is so much in that one statement: Rome is but the beginning for Dick; a fundamental belief in the virtues of higher education and of time spent away; an optimism about the future of a gifted young man.

For his part, in a brief response to O'Shea the rector indicates that he would be perfectly happy to keep Dick on for the year or so between completion of the doctorate (planned for October 1932) and his ordination (which cannot take place before Dick's birthday on 19 October 1933).[3] There are echoes here of a much earlier conversation between Brother Borgia and Kate Gilhooly when Curran ventures that Dick's age militates against going out into the world just yet. 'He will be very young even then [post-ordination] and the atmosphere here will be more conducive to study than taking up lodgings as a freelance in a convent or religious house.' There are 'one or two places where he could pick up French or German if that would be deemed more useful', but they are expensive and, in any case, they don't take boarders all year round. Better that Dick stays put in Hibernia-on-the-Tiber.

While the senior men mull over his future, Dick gets on with the business of becoming a subdeacon. In his response to McRae's January letter he does not break stride following a cursory reference to having 'receiv[ed] Sub-diaconate yesterday morning' (12 March), instead immediately professing to be 'delighted at the opportunity for studying Canon Law, useful and interesting as it will be'.[4]

And then we get on to what has been a subject of fascination (verging on obsession) for me for years and what was at the time, for Dick, a source of much anxiety and tension: the thesis for his doctorate of divinity. Over to Dick: 'The thesis I have written for the Moral Theology

Pro — on the essence and intrinsic evil of a lie. I am hoping it will pass muster.' And then . . . nothing. No commentary on its contents, no reflections on the process of calling the thesis into existence, no further details of any sort. No indication of how it will be 'thingified', as a friend of mine, Lesley Patterson, once perfectly described the process of writing a doctoral thesis. Just a quiet expression of hope that it will be good enough.

I learned the topic of my great-uncle's thesis at 9.51 p.m. on Easter Sunday 2019. For years I had wanted to know what it was. All the same, my response when I found out was unexpectedly strong. It was deep and it was personal. I have lied, and some of those lies have caused great distress. On learning of Dick's thesis topic I felt three things in very rapid succession. The first was that he had seen every lie I have ever told. The second was guilt. The third was a sense that I really needed to read and reflect on that thesis.

I know a thing or two about doctoral theses, having written one. I know what it takes to 'thingify' an idea — to take it, follow it, and use tens of thousands of words to give it shape and sense and meaning in a way that has never been done before, and to then have to let that work go out into the world. It is an odd, chaotic experience. You become deeply expert in a particular area but also feel vulnerable and highly exposed, as if the entire contents of your mind are on public display.

Doctorates are pretty cool things to have, but they are not for the faint-hearted and they are far from anodyne. Mine concerned things that were well and truly outside of my person (the reform of the New Zealand state sector), but Dick's was about something that, from a Catholic point of view, is very much within us all. I badly want to read Ricardus Gilhooly's view on the essence and intrinsic evil of lies. Not just learn the rhythm and cadence of his language, but also hold the thing, smell it and explore it as a physical artefact. I want to figure it out.

But the thesis has been lost. There is no record of it at the Lateran University, the Pontifical Irish College or the Catholic Archdiocese of Wellington Archives. I have visited all three institutions in an unsuccessful attempt to track it down. No one in the family has any recollection of it whatsoever. I have convinced myself that it sits, abandoned, on a shelf in the depths of the Lateran, but in fact I haven't the slightest idea where it is. I have resigned myself to the probability that it will never emerge.

It will have to be enough that I now know the topic of the thesis, even if I never learn anything more about it. On the other hand, courtesy of Dick's letter to McRae from March 1932, I am much the wiser on the format for the DD examination proper. 'The exam will begin somewhere about 20 June with preliminary tests on all subjects except Dogma and Speculative Moral. The actual degree will exist in an exhaustive exam in these two subjects alone, Church Tract included, and a public defence of one's thesis. If successful I shall send you word, but if not, October will find me re-attempting. Needless to say, I don't want this later catastrophe.'

Then we swerve away into mundane matters. Dick talks of the '[f]irst tastes of summer heat . . . The underclothing is being removed, violent exercise is being dropped etc. The ants and flies are waking up, growing up, or whatever they do. Time is passing quickly.' There is a sense of urgency in this letter that is missing from all of Dick's other communications. The pressure is starting to show.

There is one other curious aspect to this letter. In the penultimate paragraph Dick writes: 'Easter vac in a week's time will see distribution of paper mail, which is always kept back till holiday times.' Which I take to mean that the residents of the Irish College were only given mail during the formal breaks between study periods. (And while I'm not sure if this was still standard practice when Dick was in Rome, certainly as late as the early twentieth century — when the future editor of the *New Zealand Tablet*, James Kelly, was a student — all incoming mail was censored.)[5] Doubtless this was intended to minimise distractions and keep one's attention on the work of God that lay at hand.

McRae's response, which Dick is handed in May, is short, jaunty and designed to keep the young seminarian's spirits up: 'I don't suppose you have yet forgotten the significance of the above date! A delightful autumn day in W'gton. The lads will be on a win if it is as good in the South.'[6] (I haven't been able to establish the significance of the date, which Dick does not refer to in his next communication with McRae.)

The older man then congratulates Dick on having completed his thesis with an elliptical remark: 'You have begun to burn your bridges.' With whom or what? The land of his birth? His youth? Older clergy? It isn't clear.

And then McRae asks: 'Have you heard anything of the proposal that you should return to N.Z. after finishing up in Rome?' Just two months earlier, O'Shea and Curran had been making arrangements for Dick to stay on in Rome and then head to America or England — now McRae considers that Dick 'would benefit by having a little experience of life on the N.Z. mission before taking up anything of a specialised nature, especially if you are eventually to go to U.S.A.'

The archbishop relies heavily on McRae for advice where Dick is concerned, so it is unlikely that McRae is a lone wolf on this. I suspect that Dick's age (or lack of) is at the root of the hierarchy's change of heart. Had he been of the same vintage as his contemporaries the pathway would perhaps have been clearer.

A gossipy note follows concerning the forthcoming Congress ('Most of our pilgrims for Dublin have departed. Archbishop Redwood and Father Smyth left some weeks ago midst a blaze of trumpets'), and McRae ends with a request of Dick: 'I am anxious to get a few dozen small photographs of His Holiness. The type of thing that is mounted on the certificates of Papal Blessing, usually circular in shape, and approximately three to four inches in diameter. My object is to mount them on certificates of Perpetual Membership in the Work of the Propagation of the Faith.' A brief note in McRae's handwriting that was added to the letter at a later date indicates that the photos duly arrived in August. In the note containing them Dick explained that the ones he 'arranged to be forwarded from Berretta's are the most popular. Several others, such e.g. as the one with tiara, are generally less favoured.'

It is possible that they came from a little shop on the Borgo Pio, five minutes' walk from the Vatican and where Ema, Camille and I stayed during our own Roman excursion in late 2019. The street has numerous little outlets selling religious icons, garb for nuns and priests, chalices and other instruments of the priestly trade, as well as a surprisingly wide range of calendars containing photos of suspiciously good-looking priests (but no equivalents featuring nuns).

At roughly the same time as Dick hears from McRae, Archbishop O'Shea contacts Rector Curran to formally ask if the college will 'retain Mr Gilhooly as a postgraduate during his Canon Law studies after his ordination. On account of his youth it would seem better for him than to be a free-lance elsewhere.'[7] I have never thought of priests as freelancers.

Dick's longest letter to McRae from Rome was sent in July 1932.[8] It runs to seven pages and he wrote it from the college's Formia villa, where he is resting a week after the completion of the DD exams and '[i]n easy stages . . . demolishing the lunch of the unanswered'. Protracted periods of time are not restricted to food, for we learn that the exam 'was an altogether long drawn-out affair — a week of preliminary exams, the degree exam two weeks later, and the thesis defence two days after that'. Gruelling does not begin to describe it.

Dick is not much given to bombast, so it is not a surprise that the next sentence is underplayed. 'You will have heard,' he quietly says, 'of my success in the recent degree.' Eleven words containing the pinnacle of his life's work and they come in the third paragraph of his letter. (Twenty years in the future a local newspaper will be less reserved, suggesting in its obituary for Dick that he 'is probably the only New Zealander to have reached the degree [of Doctor of Divinity] at such a young age'.)[9]

Then the self-deprecation — 'Similar to my previous Roman efforts, it was not a stupendous success' — and finally a moment of satisfaction: 'but, when one considers all things quite a success'. In spite of the heat, the flies and the 'thrills of the Roman classroom', Richard Thomas Gilhooly of Pungarehu has completed a four-year doctoral programme in two years before the age of twenty-two. To my mind, 'quite a success' is quite the understatement.

I don't know when or how the family heard the news,

but it was first announced publicly in late July by the *New Zealand Tablet*, who had received it via cable from Rome earlier in the week that Dick wrote to McRae. Dick may not shout it from the rooftops but there is excitement, pride and a fair bit of breathlessness in the heading the *Tablet* runs with, which in descending order (and font size) reads: 'Under Priesthood Age / Holy See Gives Concession to Mosgiel Scholar / Brilliant Success Overseas'.[10] From a distance of nearly a century it is easy to scoff a little at this enthusiasm, but I find the story of this young man who is to be 'raised to the Priesthood in the Eternal City' at the age of twenty-two years remarkable.

Dick's achievement is also announced by the *New Zealand Herald* in the 'Personal items' pages of 30 July 1932. His is not the only announcement that day, nor even the most prominent. Mr D. V. Bryant of Hamilton, who has been ill, has left for Sydney for three weeks' recuperation, accompanied by Mrs Bryant. Mr Cyril F. Seaward is to be appointed the assistant manager of the Auckland branch of Dominion Motors Ltd. The winners of the New Zealand University's postgraduate awards for the arts, Messrs G. C. McLaurin and D. P. Costello, left for Cambridge University on the *Maunganui* — the former to study mathematics and the latter to read classics. For others, the world is revolving in different spheres.

Dick has already turned to the future. Taking up McRae's earlier invitation to offer his views on the matter, he sets out a plan which he asks McRae to put before the archbishop. And here we get a glimpse of a practical sensibility that is tempting to attribute to his early years on the farm, for Dick feels 'perfectly assured that a great deal of the work done for the Divinity degree is of little practical use except as a mental training. Likewise I believe that much of the Canon Law degree course (now four years) is superfluous judged on the criterion of utility.'

My heart sank a little on reading this. Emily Dickinson says: 'He has the facts but not the phosphorescence of learning.'[11] Over the years I had built for myself an image of Dick as a scholar committed to the learning of the arcane, unsullied by considerations of usefulness, so his reference to 'the criterion of utility' wasn't well received. It felt a bit as if some bleak, instrumental early twenty-first-century case for the practical application of higher learning had crashed into a pristine account of scholarly endeavour (although Dick makes the case more elegantly than most people could manage it these days).

Then it got worse, because he tells McRae that practical work in the New Zealand mission 'would teach more than books ever could'. Lurking behind that comment is the deep-seated suspicion, which you can still find in this country, that books are not entirely to be trusted, and that intellectual work is somehow not real work at all because it does not leave calluses on your hands nor always produce *stuff*. Vincent O'Sullivan captures this national characteristic beautifully when he observes of one of his characters 'that he is educated, and so at once to be held in doubt'.[12]

I find myself arguing back. In order to do either of these things (learning and working) well, surely you need an ebbing and flowing of both? And isn't there a case — reaching back to the earliest human expressions of art, literature and music — for learning and expressing things for the pure joy of the endeavour? Would it make it more acceptable, Dick, if I were to say that it is sometimes worth doing something just for the hell of it? Can you not see how banal the human condition would become if we only ever judged the worth of a thing against 'the criterion of utility'? For God's sake, man, pull your doctoral socks up . . .

I am well aware as I argue with Dick that my real issue is not with a twenty-one-year-old taking classes in Latin and completing a doctoral programme, but with the degradation of the tertiary sector in which I have worked for the last thirty years, as a university education in New Zealand has slowly been diminished to a thing considered worthwhile only to the extent that it will get you a job. Nothing wrong with that, particularly as the people responsible for this failure of imagination are the same ones who ensure that students have to rack up fees in order to get their degrees (but who did not have to do so themselves) which then need to be paid back.

Moreover, as Karl Marx pointed out long ago, work

can give meaning and purpose to things. There is that. But surely, I beseech Dick, we are not reducible to the things we do to earn money? Isn't it also the case that people need to know how to 'use their intelligence freely . . . against the default grain of habit',[13] to weigh the merits of competing truth claims and to make sense of their own and others' ways of being? Unless we wish to live in constant fear of the Other, all of that is critical, isn't it?

Mind you, I suppose that making sure people only learn what is considered economically useful is one way of stopping them from asking awkward questions of those in positions of power — although heaven knows that what we really need right now is more rather than fewer people with the wit and intelligence to put those in authority on the spot.

Then Dick relents, just a little and only briefly, and entertains the prospect of spending the coming academic year (1932–33) studying canon law at the Gregorian University and then returning home. The fact that 'the "De Sacrementis" section of the Code' is on the syllabus and is to be taught by the 'famous Fr. Capello' accounts for his enthusiasm. However, in view of his 'none too robust present health', Dick asks permission to undertake the study without sitting for the corresponding degree (a baccalaureate in canon law).

The DD has taken it out of him, and he is none too keen on further compromising his health. What he wants, essentially, is the knowledge without the accreditation. I cheer loudly inside: sounds like learning for the hell of it to me. My faith is further restored when Dick suggests that he might take 'a few special lectures, as opportunity would occur, in other subjects, such as Moral Theology and Social Sciences'. Good man — that's more like the polymath I had in mind.

Dick also divulges to McRae that '[t]he first consideration is that my health is not the best at present. Some two months before the examination, I began to lose "pep" somewhat. At the beginning of June, I was about to postpone the examination, but a temporary recovery enabled me to weather the session out. I saw a Doctor after the exam and was informed that I was run down rather much, and needed a change etc. Furthermore, I was recommended to return home at an early date, or at least to get away from the present enervating weather conditions for a holiday. However, I am already feeling improved, and intend to move off shortly to cooler spots than Southern Italy can offer. I have no doubt, but that I shall be my normal self in October.'

Now we reach an inflection point in the story. Things begin to pivot. Dick is not aware, not just yet, of how quickly his health will worsen and come to dominate what remains of his life. As would most twenty-one-year-olds, he assumes that all he needs is a holiday and some cooler weather and things will soon be right as rain. But I know that his lungs have begun to stop working.

Nadir

Dottore Luigi Sabbatucci (Medico Chirurgo) sits down to write a letter on 2 August 1932. Sabbatucci is the Irish College's doctor and his rooms are on Lungo Tevere Mellini, an elegant boulevard that sweeps along the Tiber in the Prati neighbourhood of Rome.[1] His letter is addressed simply to 'Monsignor', is written in Italian, and reads:

> Pensai di trattenere per qualche giorno alla clinica lo studente sig. Gilhooly perché aveva febbre e un catarro molto sospetto. Difatti stamane nell'analisi dello sputo ho trovato dei germi di tubercolosi. Il malato — a cui ancora non ho detto niente — desidera andare a Lugano perché spera in pochi giorni di rimettersi in salute; ma credo invece necessario che vada a curarsi seriamente in un sanatorio, o ritorni addirittura in Olanda (?) (o Nuova Zelanda?). Ora sarebbe ancora in condizione di viaggiare.
>
> Lascio a lei di decidere, conoscendo meglio le condizioni di famiglia dell'infermo.
>
> Distinti Saluti
>
> Dott. Sabbatucci

There are only four words I recognise: 'Gilhooly', 'tubercolosi' and 'Nuova Zelanda'. It is the first mention of the disease and it means that Dick is not his 'normal self' at all. Nor will he ever be again.

Here is the letter in English:[2]

> I thought of holding the student Mr Gilhooly for a few days at the clinic because he had fever and a very suspicious phlegm. In fact, this morning in the spit analysis I found tuberculosis germs. The patient — to whom I have not yet said anything — wishes to go to Lugano because he hopes in a few days to recover his health; but instead I think it is necessary that he goes to take care seriously of himself in a sanatorium, or even return to Holland (?) (or New Zealand?). Now he would still be able to travel.
>
> I leave it to you to decide, knowing better the patient's family conditions.
>
> Regards
>
> Dr Sabbatucci

Matters move very quickly. Four days later the vice-rector of the Irish College, Father John A. Kyne, writes to Archbishop O'Shea.[3] He gets straight to the point: 'In the absence of the Rector I regret to have to inform you that the college doctor has declared Rev. Mr. Gilhooly to be suffering from tuberculosis. He advises his immediate return to New Zealand. In the circumstances I have made arrangements that Mr. Gilhooly will leave Naples on the SS. Ormonde on August 28th. Mr Gilhooly is at present in the hospital of the Blue Sisters in Rome.'

'The trouble began,' Kyne tells O'Shea, 'with a neglected attack of influenza in June when he was studying for his Doctorate which he obtained. At present he is unaware of his malady and is deeply disappointed that he will be unable to continue his studies in Rome.' Kyne signs off 'With deep respect and sincere regret'. By the time this letter reaches O'Shea Dick is already on the boat home. The college's formal book of record indicates that Dick left the Irish College on 28 August 1932 '*ob adversam valetudinem*' — because of adverse health.

Ill health among college students was not unknown. Rome's reputation 'as a dangerous place for student health' was one of the reasons why the college's roll had fallen to less than half of its capacity of 70 seminarians by the late nineteenth century, and matters were not helped by the outbreak of diphtheria in mid-1902.[4] The construction of the new building on Via dei Ss Quattro in 1926 went some way to calming prospective students' fears, but for Dick things are rapidly unravelling. He has no idea what has befallen him, but whatever dreams he might have had of Washington DC or England are gone. Within the month he will be making his way back to Paterson Street and to Pungarehu.

At 11.20 a.m. on 23 August Dick sends a telegram to O'Shea: 'Returning home health reasons + Gilhooly + +'. Presumably by now someone has told him he has TB.

The mothers are always the last to know. Perhaps she did become a cantankerous old woman, but on 24 August 1932 Kate Gilhooly is a distressed mother trying desperately to find out what is happening to her youngest son. Here is the letter she wrote on that day to Father McRae:

> Having received a cable from Rome yesterday to say that Dick is coming home, we all feel anxious to know a little information as his opinion expressed in letters up until a month ago was quite contrary to the news contained in the cable. We are all delighted to hear of his homecoming but having had no letters from him for over a month, and then receiving such unexpected news we would be most grateful to you if you would be able to tell when he will be coming. Hoping that this will not put you to any inconvenience. I remain yours respectfully, (Mrs) K Gilhooly.

The deference to the clergy with which Kate ends is etched on the bones of Irish Catholics.

Homecoming

Dick writes to McRae as the SS *Ormonde* of the Orient Line is approaching Perth in September.[1] The lungs may be falling apart, but the humour remains intact: 'My cable and the Vice Rector's letter will have preceded this note. The subject of both is about to arrive.' He plans to break the voyage in Melbourne, where he will 'spend a fortnight at Geelong at the invitation of some Congress people' and anticipates, as he will be 'leaving Sydney on the "Maunganui" on the 14th October', that he will arrive in New Zealand on or about 18 October, following which he will 'call up to report and await instructions'.

There is an oblique mention of *Mycobacterium tuberculosis*: 'The journey has improved me, though I am still below normal — but more of this anon.' And there is still optimism: 'I am convinced that a short rest in N.Z. conditions will right matters.' He is met at the wharf in Wellington by my grandparents, and my grandmother Millie is said to have observed of her brother-in-law: 'He's skin and bone.'

The first of the final four letters I have from Dick is

addressed from the Pukeora Sanatorium in Waipukurau, to which he was admitted just a fortnight after his return.[2] It was written six months following his admission, and so he seeks forgiveness from McRae for his 'rather protracted silence'. Dick's shipboard optimism appears to have been well placed. He has 'very definite progress to relate', most of it concerning the 33 pounds in weight he has gained since his arrival, which are such that he is 'to all appearances well restored to health'. His time has been 'by no means irksome', largely as a consequence of the 'goodly number of visitors, including quite a few of the clergy, who have called in en passant'.

Neither is Dick among heathens, for there is a 'good sprinkling of Catholics among the patients (23 out of a total of 70) and among the staff (5 out of 18)'. Ten of the twenty-three are clustered together in Dick's row of beds, earning it the moniker 'Doulan row'. His calculations are remarkably precise, and I wonder how on earth he found this out: did he perhaps ask everyone what their religious affiliation was as a conversation starter? Did he administer a survey?

Such is his progress that less than a fortnight later Dick informs O'Shea that he has been granted a week's leave from the sanatorium, during which he hopes to see the archbishop in person at Greenmeadows, a Marist seminary not far from Waipukurau.[3] I assume that his recovery continued apace, because in the last two letters I have from Dick — short, one-page affairs — the talk is all of his impending ordination.

The brief correspondence with O'Shea (of which only Dick's side survives) in late October and early November concerns the dates of his ordination and of his first Mass, and of the eight-day retreat he is to undergo before the big day. Both letters are positive, punchy affairs, Dick indicating that he is 'awaiting with no little excitement' O'Shea's responses to his various questions.[4]

Having received the requisite papal dispensation, Dick was raised to the diaconate on 30 November and then ordained a priest on 3 December 1933. He was twenty-two years and four months old. The following morning, at 7.30 a.m., he celebrated his first Mass — not in Rome, as perhaps he'd hoped, but at St Joseph's on Buckle Street in Wellington. The news found its way to the Via dei Ss Quattro, of course, and in the notes section beside the record of the time Ricardus Gilhooly spent at the Pontifical Irish College is written in neat, cursive script: '*Ordinatus est Presbyter 3.XII.1933*'.

Silence

And here, more or less, Dick's voice falls silent. The letters cease and the archives, whether in Wellington or Rome, have been exhausted. What little I know of the remaining years of his life comes from the Sacred Heart College magazine, which, magnificently and doggedly, continues to post an update on his progress more or less every year until his death. The magazine may lack the intimacy of a correspondence, but I am grateful for the details it provides, for without it Dick would have vanished. All the same, what emerges of the years he was to spend back in New Zealand is a bare sketch of a life lived in and out of hospitals. There is no sign of the optimism with which the Waipukurau letters are infused.

Dick managed to work, on and off, for nearly a decade following his ordination. He was initially a curate at Carterton (1 January to August 1934) and then an administrator at Takapau (August 1934 to Boxing Day 1934). (While he was in Takapau, Archbishop O'Shea temporarily barred poor Mrs Rolleston, one of Dick's parishioners, from receiving any of the sacraments because her son had been enrolled — by her non-Catholic husband — in an Anglican school in Whanganui. In due course, having been 'sufficiently punished for her mistake in not influencing her husband in the right way "ante factum"', Mrs Rolleston was permitted to resume full communion in the church.)

Dick also spent a month as a relieving administrator in the Tākaka parish in early 1935, and had a short spell as a curate at Masterton (5 April 1942 to 20 December 1943). His lengthiest continuous spell of work was between February 1935 and early 1942, when he was based at Paterson Street and attached to St Joseph's parish, 'quietly and unostentatiously' undertaking unspecified 'special duties' for Archbishop O'Shea.[1] Other tasks included officiating at weddings; serving as (a) president of the St Joseph's Basketball Club, (b) vice-president of the St Joseph's Ladies Hockey Club and (c) chaplain to the St Mary's Ladies' Branch of the Hibernian Society; and helping produce the monthly *Catholic News*, a parish newspaper (complete with advertising from local businesses selling everything from gin to cakes) that was published monthly between 1932 and 1958 by the parish — and which, in October 1932, had claimed as 'yet another ecclesiastical world's record for our little Dominion' the fact that Dick had had to wait a full twelve months before even being eligible for the papal dispensation to become ordained.

While at Paterson Street Dick would also have seen up close and personal the Catholic political establishment's attempts to counter anti-Catholic sentiment.[2] Given his relationship with Father McRae, it is probable that he would have had a ringside seat at one episode in particular. In 1942 Edith Moore's anti-Catholic tract *No Friend of Democracy: A Study of Roman Catholic Politics, their Influence on the Course of the Present War and the Growth of Fascism* — replete with chapter titles such as 'The Church marches with the war-mongerers' — was seized by government officials, provoking John A. Lee to upbraid Prime Minister Peter Fraser.

Fraser, who had been born into the Presbyterian Church, responded that he was not about to countenance attacks on the Church while Catholic men were giving their lives for the country. That would have played well with the faithful; it also encouraged McRae to write to the prime minister acknowledging the government's efforts.[3]

When Dick was well enough he would also take on other roles. In 1937 he was the president of the Sacred Heart Old Boys network in the Wellington District, a role he relinquished at the end of 1939. A decade later, by which time he was back in New Plymouth and more or less permanently ill, he did the same thing for the Taranaki Old Boys, but there he lasted only a year.

For at least some of the time he must have been well enough to sing, because in an edition of the *New Zealand Tablet* from those years he is described as a 'vocalist of no mean merit'. Years later my mum, when principal of a Catholic primary school in New Plymouth, took her staff down to Wellington to pick up some new ideas from the capital's schools. In the chapel of the convent at which they stayed she met an old nun tidying the altar who, when she found out where Mum came from, remembered that there had been 'a lovely priest from New Plymouth who had a voice like an angel. He sang at dances and got paid, and he passed the money on to the nuns so they could go to school by tram and not have to walk several miles.' Good on you, Dick.

But the periods of illness became longer and more frequent. He was confined to hospital in Masterton for a period of around sixteen months from early January 1941, and from the beginning of 1944 until his death eleven years later he was too unwell to work much at all, moving to New Plymouth in 1945 to be cared for by Kate, Moll and Liz at 60 Belt Road. My mother was there, too, boarding with her grandmother, uncle and aunts for her secondary school years in what she recalls was a pretty funereal atmosphere, complete with Mass said in Latin every morning by a very sick Dick Gilhooly. (On the other hand, he also helped out with her homework from time to time.) He was regularly in and out of hospital wards and he spent two years (1946–48) in a full body-length plaster cast, unable to move at all.

Yet it is from Belt Road that there is a brief, final and entirely unexpected flurry of correspondence from Dick. Late one afternoon, well over a year after Dick's letters from Rome had come to light, I was sitting in the

Diocesan Archives in Palmerston North sifting through a box of old papers from St Joseph's parish in New Plymouth, and spotted an address, 60 Belt Road, at the top corner of a handwritten letter. Dick's youngest sister, Liz, was an active member of the parish (in 1969 she donated fifteen years' worth of earnings from playing the piano at weddings towards the purchase of the pipe organ for the new St Joseph's Church), and I assumed the letters were hers.

They weren't. They were Dick's. There are eight of them, written between April and December 1951 (when my mother was at Belt Road) and each is addressed to Father McRae. It emerges that Dick has become the Church's property manager in New Plymouth.

In brief: the Chancery in Wellington has advanced £3600 to help a Polish refugee family (Catholic, of course) into a house on Rogan Street in New Plymouth — and Dick is responsible for handling Adolf Tarasiewicz's fortnightly repayments. The Church is also considering investing in other residential properties for Catholic European refugees, McRae explaining to Dick that '[t]here is little point our building churches and schools if nothing is being done to overcome the difficulties facing those want [*sic*] to establish Catholic families but who find themselves blocked by the lack of housing'.[4]

Material matters aside, the letters also contain a few questions on the finer points of Church law. Is it permissible, for instance, for Catholics to attend non-Catholic weddings? Exactly when, if at all, can a priest drink alcohol? Dick's position on both is well towards the dovish end of the spectrum: the proscription on the former, in particular, 'seems a very stringent and severe order'.[5]

And of course there are references to health, although as often to others' as to his own. Dick expresses particular concern for his mother, informing McRae that she 'is ailing somewhat. Feels the travail of a failure of vision — result of eye haemorrhage — basically diabetic trouble.'[6] The words bring to mind another letter written to McRae nearly twenty years earlier, when Kate had pleaded for news of her sick son. This time, however, McRae does not need to respond because Dick knows exactly what is happening to his mother: she has gone blind and is dying.

His own physical condition is ever present. 'Radiologically my health appears better,' he writes in July with his usual optimism. 'While I am short of breath, handicapped in appetite and a little bit thinner, I have, I hope, a firm grasp on general well-being.'[7] Dick is a confirmed glass-half-full kind of guy. Two months later, however, there is a growing sense of resignation: 'I am only moderately well, but must persevere hopefully along my own Providential way.'[8]

And in the last two letters, right at the end of the year, Dick's dander drops away entirely. In early December things take a clear turn for the worse, and he asks to be relieved of his responsibilities because he is having 'to submit to some surgical treatment for [his] chest in the New Year'.[9] A fortnight later he writes one last letter to McRae, enclosing a copy of his will. Dick's 'Providential way' still has a couple of years to run, but he can see the end coming.

It is not so much the content of this exchange that strikes me as its tone, and the way it subtly shifts my understanding of Dick. I read over the letters again and it is clear he has lived a life. It is late in the day for him ('I am inclined to shortness of breath and poverty of appetite'),[10] but the TB has not yet swamped his spirit. There are flashes of wit: 'We are not enjoying winter's severity,' he says in June, and 'I find the most agreeable climate to be that in bed, and spend considerable periods there.' And, just as there was while he was in Rome, there is a great deal of gossip between Dick and McRae regarding the comings and goings, and trials and tribulations of their respective clerical friends. Theirs is a tight community of men.

But the relationship between the two has changed. The use of formal honorifics aside, the tenor of Dick's writing in 1951 suggests that McRae is less a mentor and father figure these days than a colleague (albeit a senior and powerful one) and close friend. That does not come as much of a surprise — Dick has been a priest for nearly twenty years now, after all, and had worked closely with McRae during his six years at Paterson Street in the late 1930s and early 1940s — but all the same I am taken by the ease, confidence and maturity of the Dick I find in these letters. These qualities were not there in the Roman correspondence, and they speak to the unfolding of a friendship that endures for the better part of Dick's adult life.

It is a lovely moment, this, when, with the late afternoon sun easing its way into the room in which I am sitting, my priest-uncle steps back into the light. To hear his voice again, after the years of silence during which he struggled in and out of hospitals and was reduced to a series of temporary administrative roles, is something I experience as a blessing. He is only here briefly, before he flickers out forever, but for the length of time it took me to read thirteen pages of his sprawling script, Dick Gilhooly came back from the dead.

Bob/TB redux

My father also had a history with TB. It killed his mother, Marion, when she was only thirty-four and Dad was just seven. The next year he also contracted TB and diphtheria, and would spend the next two years of his life in the very same ward in the Masterton hospital in which his mother had died. (Dad had also been admitted to the Karitane Hospital in Melrose, Wellington, when he was a baby. One way or another he spent a lot of his childhood in hospitals.) Fresh air and sunshine were about the extent of the treatment in 1940, so Dad alternated between waking up with ice on his bed-frame or with the sun blazing down.

Although he was in hospital he was encouraged to spend as much time as he could outside. There weren't any other children on the TB ward, but there were sick Japanese prisoners of war under guard in a separate room, some of whom would make small origami figures for him. He spent most of his time running errands, scrounging food from the kitchen and waiting to go home.

When Dad eventually wheedled Mum's family name out of her, he recalled that during his years in hospital he used to 'do jobs' for a Father Gilhooly, who in return would hand over chocolates and grapes. These exchanges between the priest and the boy — who all the while wondered where Mother Gilhooly was, for she certainly never visited Father Gilhooly — took place when Dick was serving as the curate in Masterton. It's quite the coincidence: because they were both 'consumptives', my father met Dick many years before he met the priest's niece. As Mum tells the story, the jobs Dad did were a pretext for Dick to offer a bit of attention to a boy who received very few visitors.

If disease connected my father and my great-uncle, injury caused by heavy artillery pieces linked him to my great-grandfather. In 1959 Dad was completing his final compulsory military training camp in Waiouru, attached to No. 2 Group of the 1st Wellington West Coast and Taranaki Regiment.[1] He was undertaking live ammunition training when his right arm was caught in the firing mechanism of an anti-tank gun, so badly jammed that a truck was needed to pull the mechanism back so his arm could be released.

That must have taken some time and he would have been in agony, but when Dad told that story later in his life he never mentioned that part (and I don't recall ever asking about it). There followed an ambulance trip to Whanganui Hospital, which can't have been much fun either, and then bone grafts and three months of bed rest.

My mother's father, Hugh, visited Dad in hospital. Dick's older brother was sceptical of the townie who was courting his daughter — mostly because Dad was living in Wellington but also because he was a hopeless card player with an uncomfortable propensity for helping the women with the dishes — but came around to the idea of marriage when the arm was shattered. Mangling one's forearm in an anti-tank gun is a fairly manly thing to do.

But first the townie had to convert from the Methodism in which he had been raised to the Catholicism of the Coast. I doubt much thought was given to the matter — I suspect it was simply assumed that Dad would give up his faith for Mum's. But in typically understated fashion, Dad would later write — in *The Liz 'n Bob Story*, a 200-page memoir of our family that he wrote a decade or so before he died — of the difficulty this caused him:

> During 1959 I began taking instruction in the Catholic faith as was required of all non-Catholics contemplating marriage to a Catholic partner. A good bit of each session was taken up with discussing the latest rugby news with the priest and the end result was that I became a Roman Catholic shortly before our marriage, much to the delight of Liz's parents. I did find the constant presence of Liz's family and the pressure on me to become a Catholic a bit heavy at one stage, which led to my having a wee period of doubt about our marriage but I got over that and the big day was set for Jan 9, 1960.

There is a lot sitting behind the words 'a wee period of doubt' and 'I got over that'. Again, I never asked for the details, although I wonder now — especially given that as a kid Dad had been active in (and a leader of) the Methodist Bible class movement — quite how much that cost him. He was a bit like the tip of an iceberg: much remained beneath the waterline, unseen and unexplained.

It wasn't just him. My parents were married in Pungarehu in 1960. Catholic practice at the time was to fast from midnight the night before, so my mother's mother, Millie, made sure there was a stack of sandwiches at the back of the church ready to go once the register had been signed. A day or two before the big event, Dad's father told him he wasn't going to come, for reasons which were never made clear to anyone, then or later.

My father was in most respects an ordinary man. He did not cross oceans at a young age as Andrew Gilhooly did (not physical ones, anyway), he was not academically precocious in the way Dick was (but he valued education and became an expert practitioner of it), and he did not have the interest in the serial pursuit of public office that drove his father-in-law (although he was a superb behind-the-scenes administrator).

What most interests me about him is not the stuff I was there for but what I know of him only through the stories he and others would recount. In the manner of those who have suffered, Dad's stories almost always drew his listeners' attention to the humour that can occasionally be found in situations which, from a different point of regard, take on a more painful aspect.

He was often very funny and was a fine public speaker in a self-deprecating sort of way, but if you listened carefully you could sometimes glimpse the loss that lingered behind the anecdotes and the smiles. That's the stuff I'm most curious about.

There is an example of this in the opening paragraph of *The Liz 'n Bob Story*:

> I was born in Masterton, NZ on October 24, 1934. For the first 18 years of my life I celebrated my birthday on October 23 and only discovered the error when applying for my entry for Teachers' College in 1952. For some strange reason my parents, Marion Alice and Ronald Norman Shaw named me Keith but called me Bobby, which later became Bob, so I have spent the whole of my life explaining to people why my initial is K but my name is Bob. There is a story told that the postman once brought a parcel to our gate addressed to Keith Shaw but he was sent on his way by one of my brothers because 'There is no Keith Shaw in this house.' Family folklore I suspect.

Perhaps, Dad. But I peer around the edges of those words and look at what lingers behind them: misremembered dates, a name that shifts and a parcel delivered to a boy who does not exist. I no longer find it all as funny as I once did.

Here is something from William Boyd's *Love Is Blind*: 'Home: the place you have to leave.' When he became sick my father did leave home, which was at 12 Wrigley Street in Masterton, but when he was finally discharged from the TB ward in March 1945 he did not return there. Instead, he went straight into the Masterton Methodist Children's Home at 37 Herbert Street.[2] From home to Home, you might say.

Dad remembered only snatches of life at Wrigley Street, where he lived with Marion, Ronald and their ten children — Joy, Mickey (Dianne), Ken, Don, Brian, Norma, Dad, Pete, David and Tim (Betty). American servicemen coming for meals during the war and being generous with chewing gum and birds' egg lollies. Looking up at the light from the bottom of the Waipoua River and wondering why he couldn't make it to the surface, then being hauled out by his older brother Ken.

But that life ended when his mother died on 15 February 1942. There is a photo of all ten children standing in a row outside Wrigley Street shortly before they are scattered to the winds. In my family it is an iconic image. Dad is the only one not gazing directly at the camera. Instead, he is looking intently down to his right at his younger brother Pete, who was Dad's closest friend and best man at Mum and Dad's wedding. The only time I ever saw Dad in emotional *extremis* was when Mum and I had to hold him up outside the ICU ward in Wellington Hospital, moments after Pete had died. If we hadn't done so he would have collapsed onto the lino. Mum got it, but I didn't fully appreciate then just how much died with Pete.

After Marion's death, Dad's father, Ronald, gave up his job as a trade union official and for a time tried to keep the family together at Wrigley Street. At some stage, however, he left Masterton to work on the wharves in Wellington, where he would subsequently remarry and have a second family. Much later, when Dad was at Teachers' College in Wellington, he and some of his brothers and sisters would intermittently live with Ronald and Aunty Marge, up on Williams Street in Hataitai, along with Dad's half-brothers Andrew, Ronald and Gordon.

But in the early 1940s, Dad's family splintered. Dad was in hospital. Ken went to work on the Admiral, a large Wairarapa sheep station, and Mickey and Joy went south to work in Wellington. Most of the rest of them — Brian, Norma, Don (after a spell at the same sanatorium in Waipukurau that Dick had been at), Pete, David and Tim — moved into what Dad and the others always called 'the Home', the brothers with a sense of gratitude but Norma with an edge to her voice. Dad joined them when he left the TB ward. None of them were orphans, but they were in an orphanage all the same. Two of the siblings didn't stay long: Tim was adopted out two months after they arrived and David followed her — albeit to a different family — not long after.

Dad spent eight years in the Home and for the rest of his life was fiercely loyal to the institution and those he shared it with. He cared deeply about Mr and Mrs Bateup, the couple who raised him and the other 'Homies' who lived at 37 Herbert Street, and without whose support Dad believed he would not have finished school much less made it to Teachers' College. When confronted with pity or by the insistence that surely there *must* have been abuse of some sort, Dad would quietly explain that the Home had been a home, that the forty or so kids there had been a family, and that, no, to the best of his knowledge there had been no abuse. You wouldn't press him.

Elements of my father's life as a Homie in the 1940s. Being elected treasurer of the Bible class and blowing the Sunday collection money on the way back to Herbert Street on lollies for the other Homies. Hearing the cry 'Homies! Homies!' go up at school, and racing to the aid of one of your own who was under the cosh from some other (soon to be unfortunate) kid. Resorting to nicknames — Chick, Chonk, Chow, Bottle, Big Mac, Little Mac, Julius Caesar, Bumpy, Dolly and Don Honk — because so many kids had the same name.

Staying at the Home during the school holidays while everyone else went off to Methodist host families around the lower North Island (as kids we would be heartbroken at this point in the story), and finding that you had a bedroom to yourself and there was no queue for the toilet (yay! — it ends well for our dad). Staying at the home of a Levin family one Christmas holiday and going on a trip to Taupō and Rotorua — but never being invited back (our hearts break again). Moving up through the ranks and finally being put in charge of doing the laundry, which during the winter months is the most coveted job of all because it is inside and out of the wind.

Playing 'interball national', a ball game played with no teams, rules, time limits or points system, the sole purpose of which is to get the ball, run like hell and hang onto it for as long as you can. Leading the haka for the Wairarapa College First XV, which is captained by B. J. Lochore. Giving Bob Charles some stick for not playing rugby, and being told that the chances are he will make more money playing golf than you ever will playing rugby. Wondering why your sister Tim and brother David are no longer at the Home, and finding out only years later that they had been adopted. (Towards the end of Dad's time in the Home the Wairarapa College First XV headed south to play Rongotai College. Dad was billeted out for lunch with Terry O'Neill, one of the Rongotai boys. Terry, it transpired, was David Shaw. Dad hadn't seen his younger brother since he was adopted by the O'Neills and wouldn't again for many years.)

In some respects Dad never left the Home. It was at his core. His keen sense of social responsibility and his dislike of pretension had their roots in his years of living alongside others who, in one way or another, were disadvantaged. It also shaped the kind of father he was to his own children, although not in the way you might perhaps assume. Even

Above: The Masterton Methodist Home, 1944. Dad is standing fourth from the right in the front row; various other siblings are dotted about.

Below: This photo was taken in 1957, while Dad was at Teachers' Training College in Wellington. Dad is second from the right and his brother Pete is first on the left. They were on their way to a wedding in Matauri Bay. Maurice McCarthy, the groom-to-be, was also a Homie and is standing between Dad and Pete.

if he was bruised by his years in care — and I can't see how his father's choices could not have been experienced as rejection at some level — he was not brutalised. With his own family he set about filling in the holes.

He was gentle, patient, unassuming. He did not talk a great deal and had a preference for 'moving quietly to the point of least confrontation',[3] which sometimes drove my mother to distraction.

(It also bothered inspector H. P. Henderson, who, when Dad was sole charge teacher at Mauriceville West School in 1965, told him: 'Your natural tendency to be self-effacing will need to be overcome when you move into spheres of wider influence.'[4] I'm not sure I much like Mr Henderson, because on that visit he also said: 'The children at your school are real country children. By this I mean that their emotional lives run along without many high points. It would be the teacher's duty to try to enthuse, to uplift and by his personality to bring these children out of themselves.')

He married a gregarious woman but was very good at silence. He was happiest when he was not the centre of attention. He said that he learned to be a father from Mr Bateup. I wonder that he did it so well.

As with Andrew and Dick, so with Dad. The world he moved into after he left the Home has vanished (as has he). The memoir he wrote for us is full of glimpses into that life. This one is from 1958, when Dad was teaching at a two-teacher school at Bideford, a small rural community 30 kilometres or so north-east of Masterton. It is one of my favourites, as much because of what it says about Dad's appetite for life as for the strong sense of nostalgia it evokes for a certain kind of lost New Zealand:

> There were only about 25 kids at the school and most came by bus, which I drove each day. I would go right to the end of a little narrow road, come back to the school and drop the first kids off and head off in another direction to pick up more kids. In those days, in an effort to eradicate possums, there was a bounty of 2/6 paid by the Government for every possum tail collected, so I would often stop for the children to pick dead possums off the road. They would put them under a hedge for the day and then take them home for skinning.
>
> On the last Friday of each month I had to take the bus to Masterton to have it serviced at the Post Office Workshops. If I hadn't done the correct amount of mileage for the month I would have all sorts of problems explaining to the Bus Controller why not. I soon learnt that it would save lots of hassles if I ran up the missing miles, so unbeknownst to the Education Department, the Bideford School bus was often used for pig and rabbit shooting expeditions, for weekend swimming outings and for leisurely weekend drives.
>
> On those Fridays that I took the bus into town I sometimes had a bus full of local people who would do

their weekend shopping, go to the movies or the pub, buy some fish and chips, visit friends, and then get a ride back home after the movies. That bus carried dogs, dead pigs and rabbits, rifles and ammunition, firewood, dead possums, sacks of fertilizer, cartons of food, crates of beer and occasionally children.

Sometimes I think about why I take as my origin story that of my mother's family and not Dad's. It is as if the Gilhoolys have moved in rowdily and *en masse* and taken up all the space, squeezing the Shaws out onto the margins. Some of it, I suppose, is because we lived in Taranaki for several years. Part of it is that we saw more of Mum's people than Dad's. Mostly, though, I think that the splintering of Dad's family, and the years and years it then took to put some of those relationships back together again, meant that the Shaw family seemed to have no centre.

It did not stay still in one place as Mum's did; instead, it was fluid and moved and was scattered about. Dad might disagree, I think, because from his point of view there was a centre — but that place was a Home that he (and therefore we) could not return to. His people's origin story is of a family that falls apart.

If that balance had been different, perhaps I would say that I come from another coast, from the long sweep of the Horowhenua coastline near Te Awahou (Foxton) and Te Whārangi (Foxton Beach), where Dad's father's people came — by way of England, Auckland and Turakina — to work in the flax mills. As it happens, we now have a small bach out at Te Whārangi, and the connections between that place and Dad's family are slowly revealing themselves.

The church on Te Awahou's main drag where Marion and Ronald were married; the school at Moutoa, long gone, that Ronald attended as a kid; the house on Ravenswood Place in which Ronald's mother, Charlotte (who 'was esteemed for her kindly acts in cases of distress'), died; the many Shaws who lie in the local cemetery.[5] Through Dad, I have roots in this place, too, but the soil in the Horowhenua is sandier than that of Taranaki and the roots don't go down quite as far.

On a clear day, Taranaki allows himself to be seen as we dawdle along the beach, appearing as an island rising out of the ocean. If I felt I came from Te Awahou or Te Whārangi I don't suppose I would bother quite as much about what has happened on the shores of that island off in the distance.

Death

Of Andrew's death I know nothing other than it happened in the public hospital in New Plymouth on 6 February 1923, brought on by paralysis agitans (an old term for Parkinson's disease, which he had for ten years and which meant he could not formally sign his final will), influenza and hypertension. Kate died nearly thirty years later of myocardial degeneration, essential hypertension and diabetes. Dick, who by then was just a few years short of his own death, celebrated her Requiem Mass at St Joseph's in New Plymouth. Twenty priests were on the altar that day. I imagine that they were there largely for Dick, but Kate would not have sniffed at having had the Most Reverend P. McKeefry, Coadjutor Archbishop of Wellington, in attendance at her funeral.

Dick also died in the New Plymouth Hospital, of pulmonary TB, on 21 January 1955. He was forty-four years old and roughly half his life had been spent in the grip of the disease. He was buried in Te Henui cemetery in New Plymouth alongside a close friend, Father Nolan, who died a week before Dick did. The death certificate was signed by R. L. Vosper, who gave his name to the company of undertakers who many years later would bury Dad.

There were 100 cars in Dick's funeral procession (or 120, depending on the obituary), which was described as 'one of the largest seen in New Plymouth'. His requiem, which was also celebrated at St Joseph's, was sung by sixty priests (or seventy, depending on the obituary). Four rugby teams' worth of priests on the altar is a lot of Catholic heft.

In his panegyric Archbishop McKeefry, who succeeded O'Shea as the archbishop of Wellington in 1954, suggested that 'there was no one who could say which had been of greater benefit, Dr Gilhooly's few years of active service as a priest or his long years of patient suffering, for he truly belonged to the Church suffering on earth', and wrapped things up by concluding that Dick had spent his years of illness in a state of 'perfect Christian resignation and acceptance'. It is a tidy end to a messy disease.

Dick's will — the one he enclosed in the last of his 1951 letters to Father McRae — is short and to the point. He gives £25 to St Joseph's Church so that twenty-five Masses can be said for the repose of his soul. The Wellington Archdiocese's Seminary Fund receives £500. His car he bequeaths to his oldest sister, Moll, who will spend years driving her younger and more glamorous sister around the province as Liz teaches piano, conducts choirs and performs. Dick's estate is worth just under $200,000 in today's terms, which seems a fair amount for a priest. I assume that the bulk of this is his share of the family wealth that came from the land on the Coast, and it goes to his sisters as his 'executrices'. Kate was not the only one looking after her daughters.

I've told you already that Dad died in Hamilton Hospital on 24 December 2012. We got him home that day, and he was with us, lying quietly just over there, by the TV, when we sat down to eat lunch on Christmas Day. He stayed with us for several days before his requiem was held at St Joseph's in New Plymouth. My relationship with Roman Catholicism is no longer close, but I found solace in the Church then. In rites and rituals which go down deep; in the cadence, rhyme and metre of the words; in the trance-like call and response of the Rosary; in the embrace of a community — real and imaginary — with memories that reach far back into other times and distant places. Through the Coast, through Rome, through Galbally and Kilteely and still further back into the desert and the dry. It was not an opiate, but it was a balm.

We Catholics know how to do death. We know the importance of ritual and do it well. We also know that humour is important. When we brought Dad home to the small house into which he and Mum had moved not long before he died, we couldn't get him in through the front door. After some polite hemming and hawing it became clear that the small glassed-in area that they had recently added at the entrance hadn't been designed with coffin-proportioned objects in mind. After trying (and failing) to usher him in through the door in the usual manner and then trying (and failing) to jam him in through a window, we had to stand Dad up and sort of wedge him in.

The whole thing was ungainly and completely lacking in dignity, but it was also very funny. Thankfully, someone had had the foresight to make sure that Mum was occupied elsewhere while all this was going on. Dad then took up residence in the sitting-cum-dining room for the next several days, and more than once, as we ate, drank and reminisced together, it was observed that his verbal contribution was not noticeably less than it would have been had he been alive. I remember those three or four days as a time when we 'all gathered here a little while to forestall the going there'.[1] Ema used a brazil nut to gently erase the gouges from Dad's coffin.

I have a collection of memorial cards; small, rectangular mementoes of the dead. They generally have a photo of the dead person, a brief prayer and a saying from a favourite saint. St Ambrose is what we would now call an 'influencer': 'We have loved him in life, let us not forget him in death.' The cards used to be distributed following someone's funeral, and are part of that highly ritualised Catholic world that non-Catholics find either bemusing or ungodly. Mum had a whole pile of them in her white Sunday missal, and quietly shuffling through them and poring over their details was one of the ways we kids kept boredom at bay during the service. Much later I would discover that being an altar boy was an altogether superior method for getting through the Mass.

I don't think people have memorial cards any more. On the handful of occasions each year that I accompany Mum to Mass these days I don't see kids scrutinising them the way we used to. I can see why some might find the cards twee, but I like them. They're a way of keeping your dead close; of keeping a bit of an eye on 'those who go down the close, foetid galleries of time and space without you'.[2]

Here is Andy ('Peace, perfect peace') and here Dick ('Oh God, by Whose favour Thy servant, RICHARD THOMAS, was raised to the sacred dignity of the priesthood, and thus honoured with the Apostolic functions, grant, we beseech Thee, that he may be admitted to the eternal fellowship of Thy Apostles in Heaven'). I love the way the language soars.

In among Mum's little collection of memorial cards there is a different sort of card. This one marks the beginning of a life, rather than its end. It says: 'To Dear Marion, with Love & Prayers. From Sr. M. Bernigna.' It was given to Dad's mother in Sydney, probably by one of the nuns teaching in the convent she attended as a girl. She, too, was an orphan.

We didn't get memorial cards done for Dad. Mum still looks for him each time she goes to St Joseph's.

Conversations with the dead

What stories do your dead tell you? How do you see your past? The questions Buchanan poses at the end of her *Parihaka Album* drift back into view. I recall being five or perhaps six years old back when we were living in Fiji, sitting in the passenger seat of the blue Falcon 500 as my father drives me south from the gold mine in Vatukoula to the dentist in Lautoka. Unusually, he and I are alone. The atmosphere in the car is soft, quiet. I have no idea what to say to him.

In *4 3 2 1*, Paul Auster's protagonist writes of his father that '[h]e's a man who never learned how to talk'.[1] I used to think much the same of Dad, but now I wonder if the issue isn't rather that I never became fluent in the language I needed to talk with him. Had I done so, one thing I would have asked him is: Am I the son you'd hoped for? I do know that when he went into hospital for the routine procedure from which he didn't return, he carried with him in his dressing gown a cutting of something I'd written for the

Dominion Post. These days, that is enough for me.

Later, after his death, someone I trust scoffed at the contemporary tendency to believe that unless something is said out loud and often then it cannot be. (We also live in a time when the reverse can apply: something can be called into existence simply by saying it loudly, frequently and obnoxiously enough.) All that verbal emoting, she suggested, sometimes just gets in the way. What she meant is that we have forgotten how to read the other signs, the ones that are right in front of us but which we look through because they are not put into words. I think I may have done that with Dad, and I regret it deeply.

Auster also writes of the times he spent 'rough-housing' with his father.[2] It's an Americanism, but I understand what it means — and don't remember doing much of it with Dad. I spent hours, days, weeks of my life trying to perfect the spiral punt off the left foot. A spiral punt with a rugby ball is a thing of beauty: the sensation of connecting just the right spot on the ball with just the right part of the boot and watching the leather arc off into the distance is a sensation unto itself. But I can't recall doing it with Dad. That is no longer a criticism of him, although for many years it was, one quietly nursed. Now, it is just a quiet sadness at things not done, words unsaid, experiences forgone.

But the reason Auster remembers the rough-housing is because it happened on the rare occasions when his father was home during the hours his son was awake. My father was always there. He woke us in the mornings, did our dishes every night, washed our hair (making sure we had small flannels to hold over our eyes to stop the shampoo from stinging), hung the washing out and made our lunches every day. (Glorious affairs, entire loaves of cheese bread stuffed with small mountains of Colby cheese, tinned beetroot and whatever else he could lay his hands on. They were magnificent and they were always gone by morning break.)

For years he got me up at 3 a.m. for my milk run. I wet the bed when I was a child; he was there for that, too. I would stumble to his side of the bed in the middle of the warm Fijian night and just stand there beside him, never needing to say anything. Magically he would sense my presence, wake, quietly strip and remake my bed, and gently settle me down. He never, ever chastised me. Vivian Gornick writes of the significance not of 'what she gave me, but what she didn't take away'.[3] Dad was like that. He was not a man who subtracted things from you. Instead, he offered them to you — sometimes so subtly that you didn't notice.

Some of those things come back to me as I write this. For years, whenever there was a school dance with Sacred Heart Girls' College, his Italian leather boots, which zipped up the side, would (to my mind anyway) give me a bit of a head start. He died nearly ten years ago, but his lawn-mowing shorts, which were not in great nick the last time he wore them, have only just given up the ghost and have been quietly retired to a bottom drawer at our bach at the beach. (A bit of him is out there, too — a handful of his ashes found their way to a small hole in the garden.) His running shoes are still going strong.

He loved the writer Damon Runyon (to whom he was introduced by a teacher at Wairarapa College) and Louis Armstrong (whom he saw play at the Wellington Town Hall in the early 1960s). His affection for certain aspects of American popular culture had deep roots: Mum has it on good authority (her own) that Dad was the first bloke in Wellington to wear Hanes T-shirts as a fashion statement.

He introduced me to Niall Williams, whose books are among the most beautiful I have read. Williams's novels are the antithesis of Runyon's: full of sky, space and distance. Runyon is a rackety sort of writer, but Williams knows his way around silence.

He offered me a particular way of being a man. He was calm, gentle and patient. He was, in an unobtrusive way, intensely sociable. He was good at bringing people together. He never engaged in grandstanding but had a ferocious sense of social justice. His was the kind of authority that you find in people who have no need to be in control.

I see all of this about Dad now, and know that I spent too long looking in the wrong direction when he was alive, seeing as a shortcoming in him what was really an insecurity in me. By the time I figured out that there are ways of being intimate that do not require torrents of words, it was too late.

I said that Dad was an ordinary man in many respects.

Dad — in all his Hanes T-shirted glory.

What I mean is that he did not stand out. He did not need to be centre-stage. He was not *obvious*. And I think his world was larger for that, because he was not consumed by the hopeless, endless task of fulfilling ambition. For that reason he was also an unusual and precious person. I wish I'd told him that.

And there is this. I am seven or eight years old and my best friend, Peter Prince-Wright, is leaving Fiji to live on Vancouver Island. Peter Prince-Wright's mother once told me I had a stomach like a rubbish bin. I have looked Vancouver up on a map and know that it is far away, and that I won't ever see Peter again. We form an honour guard as he and his older sister Vicky, who frightens me, leave the school grounds. I am distraught and run home down the path on which, during tropical downpours, huge toads gather. They are to be avoided at all cost because, as is well known, if you touch one you will develop giant warts. (Worst of all is when you dash into the school toilet, only to be confronted by a toad glaring up at you from the bottom of the toilet bowl.) I am in tears on my bed when my father comes in and gently hands me a cream sandwich on white bread with hundreds-and-thousands sprinkled on it.

This quiet act of kindness has stayed with me. It is my defining memory of my father and captures everything about him that was good. I think of it on the day I am married; on the days on which my daughters are born;

on the day he dies. And it is his gentleness when my best friend left that I wish to speak of on the day I deliver his eulogy in St Joseph's Church in New Plymouth.

For our part, we gradually turn Dad into a storied figure. It is a way of protecting him from his past, of keeping him safe from things that had already happened to him. Many of the stories are ones he told us of his years in the Home. Without exception these are tales of derring-do from a *Boys' Own* album: of midnight raids on the larders downstairs, launched with military precision; of Homies hurling stones at the Catholic kids walking to Chanel College on the other side of the road; of Julius Caesar being strung up from the clothesline to teach him a lesson (for some transgression long since forgotten) but managing to fall off the bin on which he was standing, nearly strangling himself in the process; of Mr Bateup breaking up a fight, putting boxing gloves on the combatants and inviting them to box until exhausted.

Years later, Mum and Dad taught at the Emperor Goldfields Primary School, in Vatukoula in Fiji. He dreamed up particularly imaginative ways of punishing miscreants (including me) that would most certainly not pass muster today, and which were clearly influenced by his years in the Home. Punishment #1: for an untidy desk — run around the field carrying said desk until allowed back inside. Punishment #2: for smoking — nip down to

Fong Lee's, purchase a packet of cigarettes and sit outside smoking entire packet. Punishment #3: for miscellaneous transgressions like calling Benjamin Traill a 'bloody bastard' (which he was) — climb up onto the roof of the school and sit there in the blazing sun until called down.

A claim has been made regarding the Home. In full it reads: 'The home has always been from its first years of existence a real [*sic*] happy home for the hundreds of children who have passed through it, where true Christian love and the teachings of Jesus of Nazareth, who so loved the children, were ever present. In fact it has often been said that the Children's Home was a more ideal home than many of the other children of Masterton knew.'[4]

I'm not sure what Dad would think of that, but he certainly stood by the Home and those who lived and worked there. The stories he told us helped us make sense of his childhood. But their real job, tacit and unacknowledged, is to reassure us that despite all that happened to him — the years in hospital with TB, and the early death of his mother followed by rejection by (and much later an uneasy rapprochement with) his father — it all worked out okay in the end. Having to decide which piece of butter to take was as bad as it got.

(Another story — one which echoes New Zealand's egalitarian myth in miniature — was that every morning in the Home one person at each table had to cut up the butter into segments. That kid got the piece that was left after everyone else had chosen theirs, so when it was your turn to cut you made damn sure that each skerrick was identical in size.)

He told us these stories, so perhaps they served that purpose for him too. God knows I hope so, but I wonder what it was really like for my father, in the gaps between the rousing accounts of bonhomie and of biffing stones at the Catholics. And there are certainly other stories of that time that we do not hear. Dad had an older sister in the Home with him, and she does not speak about her experiences with the same ease.

We found Dad in those stories, but sometimes it is as if he is reduced to them. Sometimes I feel that I never worked out how to wriggle around those patterned collections of words to figure out what else he was and what else he might have wanted to be. If so, that is a failure of imagination on my part, not his.

The story of Dick's brief time in Rome is told in a pile of letters, some exam records, a telegram or two and a couple of money orders. It is enough on which to base a series of loose impressions. His academic progress was extraordinary. I don't know precisely how many exams he sat, how long they were, or what languages they were conducted in (Latin, certainly, but also perhaps in Italian and English), but to have completed two degrees' worth of complex curricula in the first year alone is a striking achievement by any measure.

Finishing the entire doctoral programme in less than half the allocated time is stupendous. And that's before taking into account the cultural adjustment required in shifting from Dunedin to Rome, the challenges associated with life at the college and the complexities of Catholic politics, and coping with the oddity of a long lunch.

The sense of Dick that emerges from the pages he sent home is heavily influenced by the fact that, apart from the single telegram addressed to Archbishop O'Shea in 1932, all of the correspondence I have been able to track down is addressed to Father McRae. The tone and content of that communication necessarily reflects that McRae was a senior member of the clergy. And I suspect that McRae was something of a father figure for Dick, much as Borgia and Morkane may have been at earlier points in his life.

He was thirteen and away at boarding school when Andrew died, and it is not much of a stretch to imagine that at various times he turned to those three men for guidance. I don't doubt that he also sought advice from Kate, and his brothers, sisters and friends, but I have no record of this. What I have instead is a sketch of Ricardus Gilhooly that emerges entirely from his correspondence with McRae.

That profile is also shaped by what I do not know (what did Dick think of Rome?), what has not survived (letters to friends and family) and what he does not tell us (what was life under the thumb of TB like?). All of that aside, the correspondence from Via dei Ss Quattro is often marked by a sense of excitement, of forging ahead into an unknown but luminous future. There is light and hope. And then everything goes out.

Perhaps McKeefry was right and Dick did spend his post-Roman years of illness in a state of perfect Christian resignation, accepting the disease as his cross to bear. A clue that he might have done so lies in one of the letters he sent O'Shea from Waipukurau in 1933, in which he refers to 'still undergoing my travails'.[5] It is there again nearly two decades later in the reference to his 'Providential way'. But I would be surprised if there were not a part of him that wondered what might have been — intellectually, politically, religiously — had he kept well. It is clear that O'Shea had plans for him. I know this is selfish and that in speculating in this way I am asking Dick to be the kind of person I want him to be — the sort that has not only Emily Dickinson's facts but also her phosphorescence of learning.

He may not have wanted to be that type of person or that sort of priest at all. Perhaps, as his earliest letters to Morkane suggest, he wanted nothing more than to come home and serve as a parish priest in the Wellington archdiocese. His DD might not have had the personal significance that I attribute to it. I know that I am writing my story on top of his, turning him into a human palimpsest.

It's an easy trap to fall into because Dick remains oddly obscured by his prodigious academic achievements. There are glimpses of wry humour in his letters to McRae but little else that provides insight into Dick's hopes, worries, loves, insecurities. If he ever had fears about his own dying and death, he seems not to have disclosed them to the man with whom he maintained a correspondence across twenty years. Moreover, the Dick Gilhooly who lives in my head is a composite of just a handful of sources: a smattering of newspaper clippings, fifty mentions in the Sacred Heart College magazine and a correspondence comprising thirty-two letters along with six other miscellaneous artefacts.

The golden years get far more coverage than do the ones he spent dying. Few among the living remember him, and the handful of stories that have been passed down stubbornly refuse to increase in either number or scope. They are less stories, in fact, than the bare coordinates of a life: that he had a lovely voice, was a brilliant scholar, completed a Doctorate of Divinity in Rome in record time, contracted TB and came home to die.

The Dick Gilhooly I know is a sombre, focused and confident young man with a glowing future ahead of him. The brief correspondence from 1951 notwithstanding, the older Dick — the one who struggled to breathe, who lived for years in a full-length plaster cast and who died far from the Eternal City — is a shadow.

So is the milieu he was a part of. Things have changed on the Coast. Once there were fourteen dairy factories on the road between Ōkato and Ōpunake. There are none now. These days, as new corporate structures remake the ways in which farms are owned and worked, the people milking the cows are as likely to be wage labourers from the Philippines as they are to be the sharemilking sons or daughters of the early settler families.

Something is also happening in St Joseph's and it is connected to what is taking place on the land. That church has been central to my family. Dick conducted Masses there; he, Kate and Dad all had their requiems there, as did Moll and Liz. My mother sang in the church choir for many years. So did I, alongside my great friend and fellow O'Shea Shielder Bernard Leuthart. When I am at St Joseph's these days keeping Mum company I think of all these people. I remember, too, when I served on the altar as a boy, ringing bells, passing goblets of wine and small crystal jugs of water over to the priest and what have you: it was fascinating and a great deal of fun.

And yes, of course we swigged the altar wine (sweet and tasteless) and scoffed the unconsecrated hosts (dry and tasteless). At a distance of forty years I still recall Moll, Dick's oldest sister, who was a gentle, kind woman but whose requiem was held on the day the Francis Douglas College First XV played the curtain-raiser on Rugby Park. I played on the left wing in that team and it was the first and, as it happened, only opportunity I ever had to play on that turf. Instead, I was on the altar ringing a small brass bell as people from the Coast farewelled my great-aunt, Kate Gilhooly's oldest daughter.

One way or another the Church, and that particular church, has been a constant in my family's story. At the time Kate and Andrew married, the Roman Catholic Church in Aotearoa, such as it was, was dominated by the French. Mother Suzanne Aubert, Adèle Euphrasie Barbier (known out here as Mother Mary of the Heart of Jesus) and Bishops Pompallier and Viard are the best known of the French clergy, but on the Coast the roll-call of early priests included Chastagnon, Le Menant des Chenais, Menard, Rolland (on whose death in 1903 Premier Richard Seddon ordered a military funeral, such had been the enthusiasm with which the Frenchman had carried out his duties as chaplain to imperial troops during the Taranaki wars),[6] Lacroix, Vibaud and Soulas — all men of the Society of Mary, the Marists, a French religious order originating in Lyon, which arrived in Aotearoa in 1838.

The list also included Claudius Cognet, the man who married my great-grandparents in 1898. Cognet was a fascinating character.[7] He was born in the archdiocese of Lyon in 1858 and arrived in this country in 1885, roughly the time that French-speaking priests began to be outnumbered by those for whom English was a first language.[8] Cognet was in Rānana at the Whanganui River Mission for seven years, during which time and with the help of local Māori he became fluent in te reo Māori, before arriving on the Coast in 1896 to head the Māori Mission in Taranaki. Pa Koneta, as his Māori parishioners called him, was based in Ōkato, but his duties — which in addition to ministering to roughly 150 Catholic Māori included establishing the church of St Martin de Tours in Pungarehu in 1906, where my parents were married sixty years later — took him all over the district.

Just before taking up his position in Ōkato, Cognet briefly returned to France to oversee the publication of a catechism and a history of the Catholic Church in te reo, *Ko Te Hitoria Poto o te Hahi Katorika*. He also wrote a series of articles for a French magazine on missionary life in Aotearoa: his illustrations of the local flora attracted such attention that the magazine purchased the copyright to them. Cognet used the proceeds to pay for the construction of a two-storey presbytery in Ōkato (which burned down long ago), and the purchase of 'several sets of vestments . . . richer and more beautiful than any church in the Dominion could boast of'.[9] In 1908, three years after he was 'naturalised', he shifted south to another coast (donating a library of several hundred books to the district before doing so), moving to the Māori Mission in Ōtaki. Cognet died in 1912 and is buried on Pukekaraka hill in Ōtaki.[10]

The French Marists were the first Catholic priests in the country, and it was only towards the end of the nineteenth century that clerics with names like Doolaghty, Kelly and Kennedy began to arrive as the wave of 'Irish episcopal imperialism' swept around the Catholic world.[11] By the time Dick was ordained, the French were long gone and the religious hegemony of the Irish was well established. But the old centres of religious power in the west — the ones Dick was a part of — are atrophying, and new ones in the global east and south are rising.

The wheel is turning again, as the Irish slip away and priests and religious men and women from Sri Lanka, India and the Philippines take their place. Countries once colonised — politically and religiously — from Europe are reversing the tide. For some this is a story of slow decline: the demise of the institution of the family farm on the Coast matched by the disappearance of Irish Catholic priests in the churches. But it is really a regeneration story in which ways of doing both religion and farming change, the new approaches merging to create a different kind of rural and Catholic Taranaki.

St Joseph's in New Plymouth is where these two tides, the land and the Church, that have for so long carried my family's story in Taranaki, converge. For the new arrivals may be here to work the land, but they also worship their god in their own ways. You can see and hear it in the flesh at 10 a.m. Mass on a Sunday morning; in the cultural make-up of those on the altar and those in attendance; in the religious rituals the new, younger parishioners bring; on the faces of the older Pākehā folk as they try — often with much grace and considerable success — to make sense of the brave new religious world they find themselves entering as they come to the end of their lives. If you want to see the fabric of the new New Zealand being woven, go to the church in which the Requiem Mass has been celebrated for members of my family for decades.

Reckoning

The past flows through the present and on into the future. Hilary Mantel knows this: 'True. Dead men are at work. Their cause is not lost. They labour on, screened from us by smoke.'[1]

Beyond Dad and behind Dick, Andrew waits. What I know of my great-grandfather comes from the records of the colonial state. He is framed by his history but also overwhelmed by it, lost in the tumble of cadastral maps, service records and historic land titles. Whatever version of Andrew I have constructed here falls almost entirely out of his presence at Parihaka and his farming of land that once belonged to other people.

I am aware that he is reduced to these two essential elements; conscious that he amounts to little more than the hint of a person — an accumulation of inferences drawn from the momentous events he was caught up in. But for that reason it is Andrew — more so than either Dick or my father — who stands at the core of this account. Of the three men, it is the one whose outline is the most blurred; the one about whom I know the least and with whom I feel the most tenuous connection who, in the end, has the most to say. I hadn't expected that when I set out.

Two things loom largest: Andrew's presence with the AC at Parihaka and his probable participation in the destruction of the pā, and the fact that the three Gilhooly farms were part of a swathe of territory that had been confiscated from 'rebellious' Taranaki Māori in September 1865. They were just three tiny slivers of the 1,199,622 acres seized through 'a series of proclamations, laws, and regulations to make the process legal and to put Māori in rebellion at law, irrespective of the position in fact'.[2] But for a time they were our slivers.

Although it was confiscated in the mid-1860s, by the late 1870s none of that land had been surveyed, sold or settled. In time, some of it would be returned in the form of Māori reserves, but even those would quickly be gobbled up by the public trustee. Most of the rest would be purchased by the Crown through a tortuous system of vouchers, gratuities and other dubious financial instruments which collectively comprised a process that the 1880 West Coast Commission called 'simply make-believe' and 'nothing but secret bribery'.[3]

It was then sold to settler farmers like my great-grandparents in what has been described as an 'historical windfall' for Pākehā and 'historical trauma' for Māori.[4] But such were 'the materially different expectations of the parties, the lack of protection for Maori interests, and the accompanying fraud and corruption that none of those purchases met the required standards of sincerity, justice, and good faith to be valid in Treaty terms'.[5]

The Waitangi Tribunal Te Rōpū Whakamana i te Tiriti o Waitangi has pointed out that the 'confiscation of Maori land was drawn from Irish precedents. The New Zealand Settlements Act 1863 was similar in title and terms to Cromwell's Act of Settlement 1652; and the Suppression of Rebellion Act 1863 was copied, with virtually no changes, from the Irish Act of that name of 1799.'[6] The irony that Irish settlers were involved in the alienation of Taranaki Māori from their land is hard to miss. Some manage to do so, of course, including Monsignor Power, who wrote in 1925 that

> [i]f ever political despair and economic necessity . . . could drive a people from the land of its birth and traditions, to renew its institutions and its glories under different skies, these motives were present as a goad to the Irish. Possibly there never went forth to the making of new nations so potential a body of men — such a force of character and individuality. Irish ability and common-sense have been at the root of democratic institutions in every part of the new world.[7]

That is all well and good but it is not the whole story, and it does not appear to have occurred to the good monsignor that in the process of renewing themselves the Irish (and others) trampled all over the 'institutions and glories' of Māori.

Neither is it lost on me that the AC was closely modelled on the Irish Constabulary, 'infamous for its coercive mobile patrols, [and] able to concentrate en masse to pre-empt or suppress outbreaks of civil dissent, unrest or rebellion' among my great-grandfather's own Irish people.[8] These are uncomfortable parts of the elephant in my room, given that under Cromwell (who in 1649 picked up where the Tudors left off) over 11 million acres of Irish land were confiscated.[9]

In another jarring similarity, a solid proportion of that stolen land was granted to soldiers from the occupying English forces. Look at a map of Ireland circa 1650 and you will see an unsettling resemblance to one of Taranaki circa 1881. Right there are the gobbets of land ring-fenced for 'Adventurers and Soldiers', there the 'Government Reservations' and over there the white bits set aside for the native Irish Catholics.[10] By the mid-eighteenth century the little white parts would amount to less than 5 per cent of the country's total land mass, which is not so terribly far removed from the 11 per cent of land from the Parihaka Block that remains in Māori ownership today.

The first chief justice of this country, Sir William Martin, who opposed confiscation, understood precisely the lesson to be learned from the Irish case: 'The example of Ireland may satisfy us how little is to be effected towards the quieting of a country by the confiscation of private land; how the claim of the dispossessed owner is remembered from generation to generation, and how the brooding sense of wrong breaks out from time to time in fresh disturbance and crime.'[11]

One other thing. In the west of Ireland there are famine roads, 'built by the starving during the 1840s to connect nothing with nothing in return for little'.[12] Andrew, who was born a decade or so after that time, worked on a different kind of road, one along which the AC marched to destroy Parihaka. Following that invasion there was also ruination, privation and hunger, materially and in other ways.

This history cannot be peeled off and put aside. Now that I know it, it cannot be unknown. It is not enough, I find, to take refuge in the fact that as far as the law at the time was concerned, Andrew's and Kate's purchases, and the lease on the Opourapa Road farm, were legal. For behind the formal appearance of the law, the deeper, older fact of the confiscation is still there, waiting to be acknowledged.

There is untruth at work here, and the falsehood operates at two levels. The first concerns the actions of the Crown in building a legal architecture around the sale of land that had been confiscated. That is an especially devious and sophisticated form of lying. The legality of the confiscations themselves has long been an issue of contention. Efforts to raise the issue at two royal commissions on confiscated land (1880 and 1927) failed, in the case of the former because of a refusal to entertain that it was even an issue.

In the 1990s Crown counsel argued that the jurisdiction of the Waitangi Tribunal did not extend to the question either (but also conceded that the confiscations were an injustice and a breach of Treaty principles). The Tribunal demurred, and in its Taranaki report offered a 'preliminary view' that 'it appears the confiscations were unlawful because they did not comply with the statute's terms'.[13]

While it is comforting for those who benefit from the law to assert its pristine impartiality, in the case of the ploughers, the fencers and those who have been alienated from their land — not only in Taranaki but also elsewhere in Aotearoa — the law was simply the authorisation of political decisions which advantaged some and caused lasting and ongoing harm and suffering to others. Alan Ward nails it: 'The rule of law, as is often the case in a colonial situation, meant the subjugation of the native race by the settlers, for the purpose of acquiring their land, under the transparent legal guise of acts of the settler dominated legislature.'[14]

There was nothing remotely impartial about the decisions which flowed from that system, so let's not hide behind that sort of drivel. '[T]he law is not,' as Hilary Mantel patiently explains, 'an instrument to find out truth. It is there to create a fiction that will help us move past atrocious acts and face our future.'[15]

Legal sophistry also changes the original sense of a

thing and creates new meaning. In the case of the land, the authority of the state has been used to disinfect an act of theft. As any Catholic will tell you, taking people's stuff is an offence against the Commandments, liable to land you in hot water after your death. But taking possession of property confiscated from others through acts that are then legally cleansed is probably not going to produce the same outcome, because by then it is called settling, not stealing.

Legalising the disposal of confiscated land is a secular form of the Roman Catholic sacrament of confession, whereby the slate (or state) is wiped clean and things can begin anew. So is legitimising the rape of women, the theft and destruction of others' property, the eviction of 1500 people from their place of domicile and the imprisonment of people without trial — which is what occurred when the Indemnity Act 1882 gave retrospective protection to AC troops, Volunteers and others from legal responsibility for all of their actions before, at and after Parihaka.[16]

Some of those actions, it was recognised, 'may have been in excess of legal powers': nonetheless, anyone who found himself in such a position 'shall be and is hereby freed, acquitted, released, indemnified, and discharged of, from, and against all actions, suits, complaints, informations, indictments, prosecutions, liabilities, and proceedings whatsoever'. Retrospective legalisation of this sort obliterates the past and encourages historical amnesia; a forgetting of deeds done and acts committed. But that which lawmakers deem to be absent is nonetheless present, and things denied have a way of reasserting themselves.

The second level of untruth is more personal. John Bryce wanted 'English homesteads . . . established at the very doors of [Te Whiti's] house'.[17] The Gilhooly homestead on the South Road was one of these dwellings. Until I began this book I had given next to no thought to the likelihood that the family farms on the Coast were on land confiscated from Parihaka.

The fact that I have no material association with those farms is in some respects irrelevant. My ancestors established themselves there, breaking with their own history of deprivation.

Neither is it acceptable to say, as some people will, that the events recounted in this book are ancient history and we should all move on. This is simply another form of forgetting, and I can quite see why it appeals to some Pākehā. The attraction of 'moving on' — i.e. of forgetting — lies not in what is lost (and loss is what we usually associate with forgetting) but in what is *gained* by doing so.

Peace and ease of mind; that lightness of being and tacit sense of relief that comes from avoiding something you know is going to be painful to confront. It is tempting to move on — if you have the luxury of doing so. Much easier than having to reach an accommodation with a history (which is not ancient at all but in fact quite recent) of social, cultural and economic damage that has been visited upon Māori.

My friend Bernard has as clear a moral compass as I have ever come across, and works as a GP with some of the descendants of the dispossessed of Taranaki. Every day he sees the physical, emotional and spiritual price they continue to pay, down through the long years of alienation from their land. He sees the effects of colonisation: here is 'the generational distortion of [a people's] physical and spiritual well-being . . . on full display';[18] there the 'deprivation, flushed with alcohol, embattled with abuse, silenced with scorn'.[19] It is absurd to suggest that these are things to be 'moved on' from; pushed back down into the realm of the irrelevant; dismissed as existing only in the past. This is history lived on a daily basis.

Telling stories

Vivian Gornick describes the gap between theory and practice as 'a no-man's land that contains multitudes'.[1] I think about this a lot in the context of my origin story. I am one of Gornick's multitudes. I subscribe to the standard liberal position on the colonisation of Aotearoa and I am well aware of what I do (but mostly don't do) about this on a daily basis. Before writing this account, however, I did not dwell on the size of the gap between the two. I light candles to my dead in Catholic churches but had never borne witness to the past, nor dallied too long reflecting on what Andrew's history meant to me. I was close to fifty-five years of age before those things finally began to disturb the comfortable rhythms of my days.

My father's death had much to do with this process of unsettling, just as it has changed other things in ways that are still revealing themselves to me. It provided the impetus to be more careful with and attentive to the matters touched on in this narrative: fathers, sons and the land on which people stand. A close brush with my own mortality in early 2019 also played a role. The virus that attacked my cerebellum kills some, blinds others and leaves a few with lasting neurological damage. Thanks to the speed with which Ema, our friend Penny and the public health system responded, it left no mark on me at all, other than a need to stop pissing around and to get on with the business of making sense of things.

The sense-making has been complicated, partly because my stories intrude on those of others, and I am not always confident that I can recognise the point at which I am recruiting things that happened to other people to serve my own ends. Parihaka has a history of being 'done over'[2] by outsiders like me, and so while I may find some catharsis in setting things down, care is required. I need to be very careful not to treat Parihaka as an extractive industry, there to be mined for personal gain. I have learnt that we cannot 'simply help ourselves to whatever stories we like the smell and taste of',[3] and have become familiar with the uncomfortable sensation of not always knowing where the lines are.

Moreover, one of the stories recounted here is my version of the New Zealand creation story about the hard-working settler farming families who were, and whose descendants remain, the backbone of the country. For many of us this remains a powerful nation-building narrative, one of the ways in which we explain ourselves to each other and to outsiders. We're heavily invested in it.

It is there each time we talk about how down-to-earth and uncomplicated we are as a nation, each time we invoke No. 8 wire, each time we congratulate ourselves on how quickly we roll up our sleeves and get to work.[4]

Often the story is true, of course, and I don't doubt that my forebears on the Coast, and those who came after them, *were* hard-working people (apart from my grandfather Hugh, perhaps, who worked hard at meetings but may have been a little less diligent on the land).

But as with all origin stories, this one can obscure as much as it reveals. On the Coast, as in other parts of the country, what it hides is the deep story of the land that was 'settled'; the way in which the Māori world of Aotearoa was colonised in order that Europeans might 'create a new thing called New Zealand'.[5] In Taranaki the pioneering story can be told only *because* Māori were dispossessed in their own homeland: without the second the first would not exist in the form it takes.

Right there is a full-frontal collision between the nation-building tale and another, much more uncomfortable narrative — the one about colonisation, violence and alienation. And as Moana Jackson has suggested, 'the new stories never found an easy place in this land. Rather, they sat uneasily upon it like the new place names and fences that were being strung across the new private properties. They were intruder stories on a land that needed no such embellishment.'[6]

The unease and discomfort are obvious in the language of the new stories. Breaking in the land, clearing the fearsome bush, controlling the noxious weeds; keeping the premises on the Opourapa Road farm in a 'clean and husbandmanlike' fashion, ensuring that all 'live hedges' are properly trimmed and maintaining all fences to the level demanded by the Fencing Act 1908: the settler accounts (and the very text of the lease my great-grandfather signed) are saturated with the language of domination. They are also tales of the creation of new worlds through the erasure of other, older cultural and ecological worlds.[7]

But behind those words I detect fear and insecurity. It is as if the land itself were an enemy, one which, when settler eyes were no longer vigilant but were drooping or asleep, would rise up in the night. One never quite domesticated and whose rebellious tendencies had to be guarded against and constrained by fences, cadastral maps and survey pegs. These things lie deep in our colonial psyche.

It occurs to me that there should also be one last weaving together of stories, a final intersection of the account of Andrew's military service with the great nation-building narratives of this country. But it never happens. Why is it that the conflict Andrew was involved in is still largely missing from our collective (Pākehā) stories? Where are the public holidays, outsized monuments and day-long media broadcasts? Where the websites, the commemorations and the public education campaigns? How (and why) have we let people's graves and even — in the case of the Pātea Military Cemetery — entire cemeteries disappear?[8]

Why are the wars that took place here still overshadowed by those which happened far away? After all, those wars — *our* wars — were fought over the very stuff from which nations are built: land, power, control and authority.[9] The right to draw the maps and tell the stories.

The answer, I think, is that there is little honour to be had from claiming an ancestor who was part of the invasion and occupation of Parihaka, as there is in acknowledging one who was at Gallipoli, Passchendaele or El Alamein. Many Pākehā (myself included, for a long time) have chosen to avert our eyes from our own places — in Te Tai Tokerau, in the Waikato, in the Bay of Islands, and in Te Urewera, Taranaki and Te Wai Pounamu — and to search elsewhere for the best of ourselves and for our origin myths. We do so because while we can find the courage and the heroism in what happened over there, we struggle to confront the violence and the violation that took place here. We are unable to live with what lies waiting for us just beneath that surface. Not so much lest we forget, then, as best we forget.

Beneficiary of injustice

To borrow from Rousseau's preface to *Emile*, this book is 'too large for the matter contained in it, but too small for the subject of which it treats'. In it I have tried to get to grips with various aspects of my past, some profoundly discomforting and others much less so. And the more I learn, the more I realise that colonisation, land alienation and the suppression of te ao Māori are not just the defining issues of this country, they are also central to my own history. My small story is part of that big story.

What do I do with that knowledge? The position I find myself groping towards is that while I do not bear personal responsibility for the fact of those long-ago land purchases or leasing arrangements, I *am* responsible for two things.

The first is to acknowledge that I have benefited from the legacy of the three farms.[1] Those farms made things happen, and have bequeathed endowments that are both tangible and intangible. Let's start with the first type.

I am not equipped to calculate the full economic value

that the three Gilhooly farms have delivered to Andrew and Kate's descendants, but here are several snapshots that get things started. The combined purchase price of Section 44 and Parihaka A amounts to $329,698 in today's terms.[2] Just under $70,000 of that went to the state (for the South Road farm) and the balance went to Hori Teira (for Kate's land). As far as I can tell none of it went directly to the iwi from whom those properties had been confiscated.

The lease Andrew took out on the Opourapa Road farm in 1902 was worth the equivalent of around $6504 per annum to the public trustee. I don't know how much of that made its way back to the farm's Māori owners (I'm not optimistic, given the trustee's track record), nor how many people it would have been distributed among. Neither do I have access to the farm accounts that would be needed to figure out what sort of profit Andrew made from his own labours.

I do know, however, that his lease remained fixed at £35 for twenty-one years, and that even roughly adjusted for inflation, Andrew paid less than twice what his father had paid William Anderson for his lease — and the Opourapa Road property was nearly seven times larger than the farm back in Ballynagreanagh.

The family into which Andrew was born was one of seventy who leased land in the parish of Kilteely. When Andrew died he and Kate held sway over 412 acres of Taranaki farmland — which is 17 per cent more land in total than the 362 acres William Anderson owned in the entire parish of Kilteely. Andrew arrived in this country an Irish labourer and died a colonial landowner — and access to confiscated land was fundamental to this remarkable social and economic metamorphosis.

The contents of Dick's will provide the final illustration of the 'financial footholds and cushions' the three farms provided.[3] Dick left the equivalent of $1353 to the Church for twenty-five masses to be said for his soul, $27,027 to the Wellington Archdiocese's Seminary Fund and just on $200,000 to his two sisters. In these post-Reformation days parish priests are not known for their revenue-generating capacities, so I assume that these sums were his share of the family's accumulated wealth.

Whichever way I look at it, the farms provided the foundation for the economic transformation of the Gilhooly family. That wealth was not uniformly distributed to subsequent generations. To the best of my knowledge the extent of Mum's benefit was the £100 she and each of Hugh's other daughters received in his will (the boys got quite a bit more). Nonetheless, the prosperity that flowed from the land has supported the endeavours of later generations in various ways: its shadow lies behind the purchase of other properties and houses, bequests to children, support with the costs of education and so forth, on down the generations.

And each of these has its own multiplier effect, which is why intergenerational transfer of wealth is 'the most significant factor in the current socio-economic position of descendants'.[4] Far from being 'a relic of the past', the fruits of the farms are better seen as 'a living inheritance'.

This is what historical privilege looks like. There is no getting away from the connection between the dispossession of Māori and the intergenerational transfer of resources within my wider family, whatever its scale and distribution. And who is to say that those benefits would not have accrued to the original owners of the land had it not been taken from them?

Material endowments are not all that the land gifted me. Mum may not have inherited much money, but what she did get is all the other good stuff that flows from having had a place to stand: the sharp-edged sense of self; the ties that bind people together in communities and which are affirmed at each rhubarb, ham and vegetable competition; somewhere to rail against and to escape from, which is also the place you return to when other things may be falling apart. A home. The very idea of the Coast. Things that are intangible but priceless nonetheless because they help a person explain to themselves who they are and where they come from.

All of this is part of my inheritance, too, and it is no small thing.

The hardest word

I now know a good deal about the foundations on which that inheritance stands. I have learnt, too, that those intangible benefits — the sense of fit; of rightness — can be decoupled from the land and passed down the generations. So the second thing I feel a responsibility for is what I do with this new history of mine.

I have been circling around the question of apology for a while, and now seems the right time to tackle it. The history of Pākehā apologies for what occurred before, at and after Parihaka is a tawdry one: 'sorry' has been the hardest word to say, and even when it has been uttered it has often been mispronounced. Rachel Buchanan has found nine occasions on which the Crown has apologised for te pāhua (and an additional apology from the New Zealand Police Force, one of the successors to the AC, made in 1981).[1]

To a greater or lesser extent each of them has fallen short. Perhaps because the Crown presumed that an apology was appropriate (or was what Parihaka wanted) without talking with those to whom it was to be offered;

perhaps because ministers and officials unilaterally determined the content and substance of the apology; perhaps because it was assumed that an apology would heal pain, make peace and help people move on.

The ninth and most recent Crown apology to Parihaka is codified in Te Ture Haeata ki Parihaka/Parihaka Reconciliation Act 2019. The legislation makes for sobering reading, listing seven statutes the state used in its attempt to 'destroy Parihaka's resistance to the loss of their traditional lands'. In a parliamentary democracy the most powerful statements of law are those passed by the legislature. Through the mid- to late-nineteenth century and well into the twentieth the New Zealand Parliament used that power as a battering ram, assaulting Parihaka and its people again and again.

But out of a process led by the people of Parihaka has emerged a Parihaka–Crown Leaders' Forum, a relationship agreement between the Crown and Parihaka and a Parihaka Fund. These initiatives reflect a constructive process in which Parihaka was closely involved, including deciding upon the content of and ceremonial aspects surrounding the apology. Perhaps this time things will be different.

A cautionary note, however. At the time the Waitangi Tribunal was holding its Taranaki hearings, the indications were that legislation before the House, which became the Maori Reserved Land Amendment Act 1997, would end the perpetual lease scheme at some point in the middle of the twenty-first century, nearly 200 years after it was created. It won't have come as any surprise to Māori that things haven't quite worked out that way. True, the 1997 act phased in market rentals and reduced the rental review period from twenty-one to seven years. It also retained perpetual leasing.

Apologies by the Crown, whose contemporary representatives are the constitutional inheritors of Hall, Bryce and Atkinson, are one thing. But what of a descendant of a man who participated in te pāhua and benefited from the confiscation of land? What is the process through which I apologise? Is there one? Should there be?

I find the politics of personal apology fraught. It is not that I do not wish to apologise or to atone for what ocurred, or to contribute to putting things right — on the contrary, I feel those things more and more keenly. But I am unsure how to approach them. Three things in particular gnaw at me. The first concerns my motives for wishing to apologise. A generous interpretation is that I wish to acknowledge my connection to the pain that has been and continues to be experienced on the Coast.

But a cynic might question these seemingly virtuous motives, suggesting that behind them lies my *real* rationale: a self-indulgent need for absolution. That cynic might ask me: 'Who are you to seek the salve of apology, you whose history is tied to invasion and confiscation? Better you carry your burden.'

The second question is: For what do I apologise? I was not there when the events described in this book took place, and I am unclear how much meaning there could be in any apology from me for them. I worry, too, that having made such an apology I might then sneak back into the dementia wing: apology made — done and dusted. Move on. Most of all — and this is the third thing — just at the moment I am not sure that instigating an apology would be appropriate. To assume that an act of contrition would be welcomed might be to repeat the arrogant mistakes of the past.

And so around and around I go, trying to untangle things I don't fully understand. Trying to get this story right is part of the unravelling, but for the moment I accept that I need to live with and in the uncertainty and the discomfort. Given everything, it seems little enough to ask of myself.

Ending the forgetting

I started this book because I wanted to tell of a boy from Pungarehu who made it all the way to the heart of Roman Catholicism. I also needed to sit awhile with Dad. Even if at times we glanced off each other, the trick with him, I've figured out, is to accept what he had to offer as a father. It was considerable and I am profoundly thankful to him for it. As to Dick, he remains a glittering figure for me, if for no other reason than that, while I understand the deep, propulsive attraction of cultivating the life of the mind, the way in which he did this — Rome, the Pontifical Irish College, the Lateran, the DD, the priesthood — is utterly different to my own career. Dick radiates the exotic. I feel like some drab thing standing beneath a tūī in full vocal flight.

But the more I read, reflected and learned, the more it became apparent that I could achieve neither of those two things without addressing the most fundamental matter of all: where I come from. To do this I have had to end a personal silence. Buchanan talks about 'the presence of an absence'.[1] I take that to refer to the meaning that can be found within the silences and the things not said. Her words make perfect sense to me, and this book is my best crack at making present things I have long taken to be absences.

Piecing it together has not brought any sort of resolution. But it has provided a kind of clarity, bringing into sharper focus the big narrative of colonisation in which my own small story sits. It has also quickened the sense, as Avril Bell would put it, of being propelled towards something.[2] The question is: Towards what?

Towards redemption? Bell writes about the way in which the descendants of colonial settlers can harbour 'twinned desires for belonging and for redemption from the status of coloniser'.[3] Perhaps the subliminal purpose of this book is to put some distance between Andrew and me, so that I might make a claim to being someone other than a fully paid-up member of the Colonial Club. Possibly, but I don't think that is what I have done here. I have not turned my back on my history — I have consciously turned towards it and gathered together as much of it as I can lay my hands on. I'm trying to make sense of it, not seek redemption from it.

Towards what, then? I think the answer lies in John Newton's reflections on the process of becoming Pākehā.[4] I like the use of 'becoming' (rather than the more common 'being'), because that clarifies that you need to figure out what it means to be of and from a colonial settler family, particularly one implicated in the things described in these pages. That understanding doesn't just fall into your lap (well, it certainly hasn't into mine) — it has to be actively sought and pieced together. All the time. This is a sort of politics of failure, I suppose, because I am always in the process of getting there and never arriving.[5] But I find the business of figuring this out fulfilling and generative. I realise that arriving is not the point.

I am also coming to understand that I need to enter 'into a relationship with colonization rather than being redeemed from implication in it'.[6] The words 'with' and 'from' are the critical ones in that sentence, because they speak to apprehending my personal association with colonisation — a word that sounds like it belongs at the level of high politics but which, at the really pointy end, sits down at the dinner table and makes itself at home — rather than ignoring it.

And something is going on with time. Robert Macfarlane talks of walking 'in search of a route into the past, only to find myself delivered again and again to the contemporary'.[7] Writing this I find that the different pasts are beginning to overlap, both with each other and with the present. Fifth November 1881 was a signal event, but Mrs Okeroa's treatment at the hands of the Lands and Survey Department three score and ten years later made it 'not past', and the work that Bernard does every day makes it very present indeed.

So it transpires that the past is not, in fact, another country at all — it is the place we inhabit on a daily basis. But the experience is not equal. The challenges still faced by those whose worlds were shattered by land confiscations and the good fortune I continue to enjoy are two sides of a colonising coin that was issued a century and a half ago but which remains legal tender.

Taranaki is the place I reach for when people ask me where I am from. Although I have lived on the Coast only briefly, that is where my roots are — and I have found that roots are inclined to come with you when you move.[8] For the better part of my life I have told myself a particular story about the Coast and my place on it. But as I assembled the old maps, the certificates of title and the histories; as the scraps and shards of the past quietly drifted together and a fuller truth came slowly into focus, I became aware of the silence that has had to be maintained in order to keep that comfortable story of mine from falling apart.

Behind that hush the deep stories in the land — the ones from before the arrival of the AC and the settlers — have been gathering, their murmurings growing louder as the old certitudes have begun to crumble away. These stories have 'the power to haunt and to disturb'.[9] They are of something other, older, although I do not think that

I would be able to fathom them. And as I am learning, some things are simply not mine to know, and sometimes disappointment is the right thing to look for.[10]

Anyway, I have my own work to be getting on with. The things uncovered in this book will always be with me. Well before the French priests, the backward cows, the Roman thesis, the TB, the Home, the mangled arm and the cream sandwiches there were the AC, the confiscations and the West Coast lease scheme. They are by no means all that my heritage amounts to but they are part of where I come from and what I am now, and I need to make them my own.

'Unless the past and the future [are] made part of the present by memory and intention', Le Guin once said, 'there [is], in human terms, no road, nowhere to go.'[11] So if I want to continue to walk on the Coast, best I get my story straight. Best I end the forgetting.

Notes

List of abbreviations used

AC	Armed Constabulary
AJHR	*Appendices to the Journals of the House of Representatives*
BD	Bachelor of Divinity
CAWA	Catholic Archdiocese of Wellington Archives
DD	Doctor of Divinity
HCSA	Holy Cross Seminary Archives
LINZ	Toitū te Whenua Land Information New Zealand
NZPD	*New Zealand Parliamentary Debates*
PNDA	Palmerston North Diocesan Archives
STL	Licentiate of Sacred Theology
Wai 143	*Taranaki Report: Kaupapa Tuatahi* (Wellington: Waitangi Tribunal, 1996)

Prologue

1 Ursula K. Le Guin, 'Introduction to Rocannon's World', in *Ursula K. Le Guin: Hainish Novels & Stories*, Vol. 1, ed. Brian Attebery (New York: Library of America, 2017), xi–xviii.

2 The quote is from lines 75–76 of Stoppard's script, and are pored over in detail in John Fleming's 2013 article '"It's wanting to know that makes us matter": Epistemological and Dramatic Issues in Tom Stoppard's *Arcadia*', *Miranda* [online]: http://journals.openedition.org/miranda/5551

Start here

1 Rachel Buchanan, *The Parihaka Album: Lest We Forget* (Wellington: Huia, 2009), 39.

2 The quote is from 'Trumpeters', one of the stories in *Owen Marshall: Selected Stories*, ed. Vincent O'Sullivan (Auckland: Random House, 2008), 206. But unlike Trumpeter, who 'advanced on to language as he would an untried bridge — with caution and reserve' (p. 206), Dad was entirely comfortable with words, having spent his life in and around them. It's just that they came to him a little more slowly as he aged.

3 A cousin, Judi Altinkaya, tells some beautiful stories of the women on my maternal grandmother's side of the family in her history of the Jones family, *A Family Successfully Raised* (Wellington: Judi Altinkaya, 2013).

4 My friend Avril Bell has a lot to say — all of it worth reading — about the unsettling of settler accounts in her book *Relating Indigenous and Settler Identities: Beyond Domination* (Basingstoke: Palgrave Macmillan, 2014).

5 Many years later I was at a reunion for Francis Douglas Memorial College, where I went to secondary school. My youngest daughter, Rosalie, and I were dawdling around the corridors looking at the newspaper clippings that had been put together to mark the event. There was a cutting of me in full Tin Man regalia belting out 'If I Only Had a Heart'. Some wit had scribbled out 'Heart' and inserted 'Brain'. Rosalie thought that was hilarious. I may have been a bit more defensive.

6 The quote is from Niall Williams's *History of the Rain* (London: Bloomsbury, 2014).

7 Ashleigh Young wrote this in an essay published on the *Guardian* website on 30 December 2019, https://www.theguardian.com/world/2019/dec/31/aotearoa-is-at-last-finding-its-voice-helping-us-heal-after-a-year-of-tragedy.

5 November 1881

1 Rachel Buchanan, 'Beating Shame: Parihaka and the Very Long Sorry', *Te Pouhere Kōrero* 6 (2012): 14.

2 Rachel Buchanan and Maria Tumarkin, 'Bread and Breadth: Two Reflections on the Ethics of (Doing) History', *Australian Humanities Review* 52 (2012): 85.

3 Anderson was an Englishman from Devonshire and the major lessor in Kilteely Parish. He owned at least four 'townlands' (a small geographical division of land) in the parish, one of which was Ballynagreanagh. In total he owned over 1500 acres in the counties of Limerick and Cork.

4 In the nineteenth century 'rescue of cattle' was a criminal offence in New Zealand — with which, in 1884, one person was charged but not convicted (*AJHR* 1885 H-4, p. 4). Used in this sense, perhaps 'rescue' is akin to 'rustling' or 'theft'.

5 David Fitzpatrick, *Irish Emigration, 1801–1921* (Dublin: Economic and Social History Society of Ireland, 1984), 30.

6 Hugh Gilhooly remained in Ballynagreanagh and died, a widower, of 'senile decay' in 1896 at the age of eighty-four. He appears to have been the last of the Gilhoolys in the townland: the 1901 census lists no Gilhoolys in Ballynagreanagh.

7 *AJHR* 1874, D-2, p. 64.

8 The name is also fairly rare in Ireland itself. Gilhooly appears just 390 times in the 1901 Irish census, the first for which complete records exist. 'Fleming', however, which was my great-grandmother's family name, is there 5875 times.

9 Jock Phillips and Terry Hearn, *Settlers: New Zealand Immigrants from England, Ireland and Scotland 1800–1945* (Auckland: Auckland University Press, 2008), 43. Towards the end of the nineteenth century around half of all West Coast miners had been born in Ireland.

10 *AJHR* 1892, D-3a, p. 18.

11 Phillips and Hearn, *Settlers*, 43.

12 Angela McCarthy, 'Personal Letters and the Organisation of Irish Migration to and from New Zealand, 1848–1925', *Irish Historical Studies* 33, no. 131 (2003): 297–319.

13 Heather McNamara, '*The New Zealand Tablet* and the Irish Catholic Press Worldwide, 1898–1923', *New Zealand Journal of History* 37, no. 2 (2003): 157–58.

14 Keith Sinclair, *A History of New Zealand* (London: Penguin, 1959), cited in Phillips and Hearn, *Settlers*, 10.

15 *AJHR* 1875, D-2, p. 68. The sectarianism continued after death. Many cemeteries in this country have separate Catholic and Protestant sections. Andrew and Kate Gilhooly lie in the Catholic section of the Ōkato cemetery, with their Protestant friends and neighbours resting on the other side of the small drive into the cemetery.

16 *AJHR* 1870, B-2, p. 19.

17 *AJHR* 1874 D-1A, p 3.

18 Ibid., p. 4.

19 Much has been written about Parihaka. This section draws heavily on the Waitangi Tribunal's *Taranaki Report: Kaupapa Tuatahi* (Wai 143). Other sources include Rachel Buchanan, *The Parihaka Album: Lest We Forget* (Wellington: Huia, 2009); Rachel Buchanan, *Ko Taranaki Te Maunga* (Wellington: Bridget Williams Books, 2018); Danny Keenan, *Te Whiti o Rongomai and the Resistance of Parihaka* (Wellington: Huia, 2015); Hazel Riseborough, *Days of Darkness: The Government and Parihaka, Taranaki, 1878–1884* (Auckland: Penguin, 2002); and Dick Scott, *Ask That Mountain: The Story of Parihaka* (Auckland: Heinemann & Southern Cross, 1975). For a rather different version of that history, see William K. Howitt's 1945 *A Pioneer Looks Back* and the 1947 follow-up *A Pioneer Looks Back Again* (both published in Auckland by Oswald-Sealy). In the first, Howitt dismisses the events at Parihaka as 'the Te Whiti disturbances' (p. 47), while in the second they are characterised as 'a general cleaning up of undesirables' (p. 168) by 'tanned, brawny chaps' (p. 167). The 1945 version has been borrowed just six times from Massey University's library; there is no indication that the later edition has ever been issued (other than to me).

20 Wai 143, p. 200; Te Ture Haeata ki Parihaka/Parihaka Reconciliation Act 2019, p. 14.

21 Keenan, *Te Whiti o Rongomai*, 72.

22 Wai 143, p. 213.

23 Keenan, *Te Whiti o Rongomai*, 69.

24 *AJHR* 1882, G-5b, p. 1.

25 Keenan, *Te Whiti o Rongomai*, 80.

26 Riseborough, *Days of Darkness*, 69. Both Māori and the Crown considered the Waingongoro an important boundary. For the former

it was, by the early 1870s, considered the northern limit to settler expansion; at least in the mind of settlers in the area, the latter had given an undertaking that no Māori 'rebel' would be allowed south of the river (Wai 143, p. 168).

27 Riseborough, *Days of Darkness*, 81.

28 Wai 143, p. 92. There is a view that Governor George Grey used this second conflict to justify his assertions of a threat from Waikato iwi. See Richard Taylor, 'The Strategy of War', in *Contested Ground: Te Whenua I Tohea: The Taranaki Wars 1860–1881*, ed. Kelvin Day (Wellington: Huia, 2010), 72.

29 Wai 143, p. 226.

30 Ruakere Hond, 'The Concept of Wānanga at Parihaka', in *Parihaka: The Art of Passive Resistance*, eds Te Miringa Hohaia, Gregory O'Brien and Lara Strongman (Wellington: Victoria University Press, 2005), 83.

31 Riseborough, *Days of Darkness*.

32 Peter Low and Alisa Smith, 'Nonviolence at Parihaka during New Zealand's Colonial Period', in *Legacy and Future of Nonviolence*, eds Mahendara Kumar and Peter Low (New Delhi: Rajagopal PV/Gandhi Peace Foundation, 1996), 158–70. That article is cited by Tonga Karena, 'Reclaiming the Role of Rongo: A Revolutionary and Radical Form of Nonviolent Politics', in *Revolutionary Nonviolence: Concepts, Cases and Controversies*, eds Richard Jackson, Joseph Llewellyn, Griffin Manawaroa Leonard, Aidan Gnoth and Tonga Karena (London: ZED Books, 2020), 200–23.

33 Wai 143, p. 230. The arrests did not play well in London, with one MP in the Commons, Charles Bradlaugh, asking the under-secretary of state for the colonies to 'at once take some action on behalf of these men, who are all, I am credibly informed, absolutely ignorant of the English language, and utterly defenceless against this wrong' (*AJHR* 1881, G-7, p. 2).

34 *NZPD* 1879, vol. 34, p. 621.

35 Ibid., p. 797.

36 Buchanan, *Lest We Forget*. Scott Hamilton's 2018 *Ghost South Road* (Hamilton: Atuanui Press) tells the story of another military road, the Great South Road, which was constructed to enable imperial troops to invade the Waikato. The South Road in Taranaki was often also

called the Great South Road in press reports of the time, although on cadastral maps it is clearly marked as the South Road.

37 Te Ture Haeata ki Parihaka 2019, p. 15.

38 *AJHR* 1882, G-1, p. 10.

39 The South Island is often referred to as 'Middle Island' in the parliamentary record of the time (for example, see *AJHR* 1884, G-3, which shows 'the Number of Aboriginal Natives resident in each Provincial District of the Middle and Stewart Island').

40 Wai 143, p. 202. That view prompted a member of the Legislative Council, Hon. R. Hart, to fulminate (in a speech that took an hour and a half to deliver and which consumed fifteen columns in Hansard) that the commissioners must have been 'suffering under a mesmeric exaltation, causing them to put judgment and memory in the background, and let imagination have its sway' (*AJHR* 1882, G-5a, p. 10).

41 Wai 143, p. 204.

42 Riseborough, *Days of Darkness*, 89.

43 *NZPD* 1879, vol. 34, p. 797.

44 Wai 143 I17, p. 255. There were fifty-seven sections in total in Block 12.

45 *AJHR* 1882, H-14, p. 2.

46 *AJHR* 1883, A-4, p. 5.

47 Wai 143, p. 206.

48 Hazel Riseborough, 'A New Kind of Resistance', in *Contested Ground*, 249.

49 Hazel Riseborough, 'Te Pāhuatanga O Parihaka', in *Parihaka: The Art of Passive Resistance*, 37.

50 Wai 143, p. 206.

51 Te Ture Haeata ki Parihaka 2019, p. 10.

52 *AJHR* 1882, G-1, p. 10.

53 Richard Hill is an authority on the Armed Constabulary. His publications include *The Colonial Frontier Tamed: NZ Policing in Transition: 1867–1886* (1989), which is the second volume of his monumental *History of Policing in New Zealand* (Wellington: Department of Internal Affairs); 'Armed Constabulary', in *The Oxford Companion to New Zealand Military History*, ed. Ian McGibbon

(Auckland: Oxford University Press, 2000), 32–36; and 'War and Police: The Armed Constabulary in the Taranaki Wars', in *Contested Ground.*

54 Hill, *The Colonial Frontier Tamed,* 1. The AC did lots of other things. Its 1881 annual report indicates that constables 'serve all jury summons; take the census, and collect agricultural statistics; report all applications for charitable aid; attend as orderlies at the Supreme, District, and Magistrates' Courts; report upon the estates of lunatics and deceased persons; inquire into the circumstances of people having children in the Industrial School; . . . and, in the Canterbury District, enforce the provisions of the Contagious Diseases Act' (*AJHR* 1881, H-18, p. 1).

55 Hill, *The Colonial Frontier Tamed,* 1.

56 Ibid., 33.

57 Here are some of the offences committed by people arrested by constables in 1881: Absconding from Industrial Schools; Auctioneers Ordinance, breaches of; Bawdy-house, keeping; Cattle-maiming; Damaging constables' uniform; Diseased Sheep Act, offences against; Employment of Females Act, offences against; Furious driving; Lunacy; Sly-grog selling (*AJHR* 1881, H-18, p. 4). Interestingly, no one was charged with bawdy-house keeping in 1884, which was an improvement of one on the previous year's efforts (*AJHR* 1885 H-4, p. 3).

58 Hill, *The Colonial Frontier Tamed,* 306, 308.

59 Ibid., 325.

60 Hill, 'Armed Constabulary', 34, 295.

61 In her note, probably written in the early 1980s, my Great-aunt Liz indicated that Andrew had served in the 'Police, Kumara'. This seems not to have been the case, because Archives New Zealand Te Rua Mahara o te Kāwanatanga have no record of him either there or in Hokitika at that time. Moreover, there wasn't even a police station in Kumara in the mid-1870s. In a letter dated 30 August 1876 — the year before Andrew joined the AC — the provincial superintendent based in Hokitika sought funding for the construction of a police station in Kumara, informing the minister of justice that '[t]he want of local offices including Police Station, Court House, Lock up etc is now beginning to be severely felt and I have received a Petition signed by

over three hundred inhabitants praying that immediate steps may be taken for their establishment'. His request for £1000 was agreed to at a meeting of the cabinet the very next day.

62 Wai 143, p. 8.

63 Ibid.

64 Wai 143 I17.

65 Nigel Prickett, *The Archaeology of a Military Frontier: Taranaki, New Zealand, 1860–1881* (PhD thesis, University of Auckland, 1981).

66 The AC's own version of events at Parihaka is found in a report by Lieutenant Colonel Roberts, the commanding officer of the Taranaki District, which is part of its 1882 annual report (*AJHR* 1882, H-14, pp. 2–4). It is brief and laudatory, and comprises language that veers from the patronising ('In August the Maoris went to work clearing, fencing, and cultivating in the most independent manner') to the intimidating ('"A" Company was composed of men temporarily selected for special duty from all the companies on account of their size and strength, and formed a very imposing body'). Roberts 'cannot report too favourably on the exemplary conduct of, and good feeling displayed between, all branches of the colonial forces while in the district'. So that's good.

67 Quoist's words, which are from his *Prayers of Life* (Dublin: Gill & Macmillan, 1963), 8, appear as an epigram in Chapter 6 of Riseborough, *Days of Darkness*.

68 Buchanan, 'Beating Shame', 11.

69 Buchanan, *The Parihaka Album*.

70 Goring, who had fought in the invasion of the Waikato and against Tītokowaru at both Te Ngutu-o-te-manu and Moturoa, will crop up again a little later in this story. Andrew would have first encountered him at the AC's redoubt in Ōpunake, where Goring had been based since his transfer from Ōpōtiki in 1879 (and from which he carried out the first arrests of Tohu and Te Whiti's ploughers in mid-1879). Goring, who spoke te reo Māori, commanded the AC garrison at Cape Egmont which my great-grandfather was part of and which guarded the erection of the lighthouse. He came from good stock: his family were descended from Anglo-Irish aristocracy and his father was clerk of the Executive Council. On 25 November 1880 Goring's sister-in-law (some

reports have her as his niece), Mary Dobie — who beautifully sketched Te Whiti and Parihaka — was murdered not far from the Ōpunake redoubt. David Hastings' 2015 book *The Many Deaths of Mary Dobie: Murder, Politics and Revenge in Nineteenth-Century New Zealand* (Auckland: Auckland University Press) tells her story.

71 Hill, *The Colonial Frontier Tamed*, 330.

72 Prickett, *The Archaeology of a Military Frontier*.

73 The quotations in this paragraph are taken from *AJHR* 1882, G-3, p. 1; *AJHR* 1882, H-14, p. 4.

74 *AJHR* 1885, G-4, pp. 1–9.

75 Ibid., p. 4.

Putting things off

1 *AJHR* 1885 H-4, p. 1.

2 For a fascinating commentary on this project see Lieutenant Colonel Boddam's *Report on the Construction of the Harbour Defences of New Zealand* (*AJHR* 1887[1] vol. 1, H-12, pp. 7–9).

3 The panic is covered in detail in Peter Cooke, *Defending New Zealand: Ramparts on the Sea 1840–1950s* (Wellington: Defence of New Zealand Study Group, 2000).

4 *AJHR* 1887(2) vol. 1, A-7, p. 2. According to Cooke (*Defending New Zealand*, 49), the 'tour of spoliation' referred to a Russian plan from 1878 which contemplated naval raids on Australian ports.

5 Richard Hill, 'War and Police: The Armed Constabulary in the Taranaki Wars', in *Contested Ground: Te Whenua I Tohea: The Taranaki Wars 1860–1881*, ed. Kelvin Day (Wellington: Huia, 2010), 35.

6 The artillery garrisons were in Auckland (No. 1 Battery), Wellington (No. 2 Battery), Lyttelton (No. 3 Battery) and Dunedin (No. 4 Battery). See Cooke, *Defending New Zealand*, 172.

7 Forster Goring's military career was also curtailed by failing eyesight. On leaving the services (with the rank of colonel) he and his wife Bertha lived out their lives as orchardists in Whāngarei (David Hastings, *The Many Deaths of Mary Dobie: Murder, Politics and Revenge in Nineteenth-Century New Zealand* [Auckland: Auckland University Press, 2015]).

Land

1 *Hawera & Normanby Star*, 16 September 1893.

2 Land sales began at the Land Office in New Plymouth on 8 September 1881, but the dates on which the individual sections were sold are not marked. It is likely that Andrew purchased Section 44 from someone else, because on his historic title is also recorded a previous title. Unfortunately, Toitū te Whenua Land Information New Zealand (LINZ) can find no record of that earlier title, so I cannot establish when Section 44 first passed out of te ao Māori.

3 Neill Atkinson, *Adventures in Democracy: A History of the Vote in New Zealand* (Dunedin: Otago University Press, 2003). Andrew would have qualified to vote as early as the 1879 election, two years after he had joined the AC, but whether his name is spelt Gillooly or Gilhooly I can find no sign of him on the relevant rolls in the Dunedin or Taranaki areas before 1893.

4 This detail is from *Summary of what happened to the land within the Parihaka Block — 1882 onwards* (Wai 143 I4), an unattributed document prepared for the Waitangi Tribunal's Taranaki hearings and which staff at the Tribunal generously sent me.

5 It is tempting to attribute this to avarice, but it may have been a result of incompetence. In 1882 William Fox, a West Coast commissioner, felt obliged to bring the sorry state of the quality of the surveying in Taranaki to the attention of the governor. Fox bemoans the shortage of professionals, conceding that the work, 'in the hands of too often incompetent persons, is got through sufficiently to enable the land to be occupied, though in a rough-and-ready manner, which insures [*sic*] a large proportion of error, and often results in nearly all the work having to be corrected and done over again at a future day' (*AJHR* 1882, G-5, p. 4).

6 Wai 143 I4, p. 3.

7 Ibid., p. 4.

8 *Alienation of land within the Parihaka Block* (Wai 143 I17, p. 273). This remarkable piece of research, prepared by Marlene Benson and Te Miringa Hohaia for the Waitangi Tribunal's Taranaki hearings, outlines the history of each of the forty separate grants the Crown

made to Māori within the entire Parihaka Block (which amounted to just 21,482 of the 45,000 acres the Crown initially promised to return). It also itemises the main means by which almost all of that land was subsequently alienated, ranging from Crown purchases to the amalgamation of leases. It is an extraordinary and deeply unsettling document.

9 Wai 143 I17, pp. 272–73.

10 Hazel Riseborough, 'A New Kind of Resistance', in *Contested Ground: Te Whenua I Tohea: The Taranaki Wars 1860–1881*, ed. Kelvin Day (Wellington: Huia, 2010), 241.

11 By 1883 the state had set aside 55,699 acres in 'Lands reserved exclusively for Natives' (*AJHR* 1883, G-7b, p. 1). Only 2741 acres were classified as 'inalienable reserves', however; the rest were 'alienable reserves' and in time were duly alienated.

12 Danny Keenan, *Te Whiti o Rongomai and the Resistance of Parihaka* (Wellington: Huia, 2015).

13 Te Miringa Hohaia, Gregory O'Brien and Lara Strongman, eds, *Parihaka: The Art of Passive Resistance* (Wellington: Victoria University Press, 2005); Rachel Buchanan, *The Parihaka Album: Lest We Forget* (Wellington: Huia, 2009).

14 Buchanan, *The Parihaka Album*, 177.

15 Rachel Buchanan, *Ko Taranaki Te Maunga* (Wellington: Bridget Williams Books, 2018), 63.

16 Wai 143, p. 258. This occurred through the West Coast Reserves and West Coast Settlement Reserve legislation and their various amendments down the years.

17 *AJHR* 1907, vol. 3, G-1c, pp. 13–14.

18 *AJHR* 1888, G-5, p. 8.

19 Wai 143, p. 246.

20 Wai 143 I17.

21 Ibid., p. 214.

22 Ibid., p. 188.

23 Wai 143 I4, p. 7. A number of Māori refused on principle to accept rents for land they owned but were legally excluded from. Further, one of

the pernicious effects of the forced individualisation of title was that a piece of land could have many owners. In 1971, for instance, Section 4 of the Cape Survey District Block 12, which comprised just 21 acres, had eighteen owners, each of whom would have received vanishingly small returns on their share in the land (Wai 143 I17).

24 Wai 143 I17, p. 206.

25 Wai 143 I4, pp. 7–8. I have transcribed the letter exactly as it appears in the historical record. My friend Janine Hayward, professor of politics at the University of Otago, generously read an early draft of this book and pointed out that at the time this letter was written Māori land was being compulsorily acquired for public works (such as roading) and then Māori were being charged rates. In other words, they were paying rates for roads built on land that was still in Native title.

26 Section 9.3 of the Tribunal's Taranaki report provides detail on the lease scheme (and there is more in its 2001 report, *Taranaki Māori, Diary Industry Changes, and the Crown*).

27 Buchanan's account (*The Parihaka Album*, 182–84) is based on the work of Te Miringa Hohaia and Marlene Benson, whose case study *Cape Egmont Lighthouse Reserve* was presented to the Waitangi Tribunal Te Rōpū Whakamana i te Tiriti o Waitangi during its Taranaki hearings.

28 The location of this small piece of land suggests to me that this is the same rangatira, Te Whetu Moeatu, who had an exchange with one of the Fleming brothers regarding fences in 1885. If so, it is likely that James was the Fleming involved in that earlier incident, because his farm (Section 2 of Block 12) was immediately adjacent to the land Te Whetu Moeatu leased in 1887.

29 Wai 143 I17, p. 275.

30 Buchanan, *The Parihaka Album*, 184.

31 T. Shoebridge, *The Alienation of Maori Land in the Ohura South Block* (Wai 903 A67, 2004, p. 13).

32 *AJHR* 1908 G-1F, p. 1.

33 Ibid., p. 2.

34 Wai 143 I17, p. 6.

35 Wai 143, p. 13.

36 'Weight of the Planets' is from Aldous Harding's third album, *Designer* (4AD, 2019).

37 Some of the detail about the farms is from the records that sit behind Hohaia and Benson's *Alienation of land within the Parihaka Block*. The ones I'm most interested in are Wai 143 I17 and Wai 143 I17(f).

38 I'm grateful to Frank Hofmans for explaining to me where the farm was. Frank's parents, Margaret and Cor (Cornelius Hofmans, a Dutchman), took over the lease from Margaret's father Andy (Kate and Andrew's son), and Frank grew up on the farm.

39 Wai 143 I17, p. 187.

40 Ibid., p. 188.

41 By the mid-1990s over 70 per cent of the Parihaka reserves had been sold. There wasn't much land left to live on, let alone to make a living from.

42 It is fashionable these days to think that individualism was created in the 1980s by neoliberalism's cheerleaders — but the Native Land Court was at it a century earlier. This is the court, mind you, that was established by legislation about which it was said that 'if the Legislature had desired to create a state of confusion and anarchy in Native-land titles it could not have hoped to be more successful than it has been' (*AJHR* 1891 G-1, p. x).

43 Depending on the source, Taylor was either a whaler or a ship's carpenter. The detail regarding Hori Teira comes from several sources. The most significant is an early draft of Tonga Karena's chapter 'Reclaiming the Role of Rongo: A Revolutionary and Radical Form of Nonviolent Politics', in *Revolutionary Nonviolence: Concepts, Cases and Controversies*, eds Richard Jackson, Joseph Llewellyn, Griffin Manawaroa Leonard, Aidan Gnoth and Tonga Karena (London: ZED Books, 2020), 200–23. Karena is a descendant of Hori Teira. Erin Griffin's *Tales of Te Namu and Hori Teira*, published in 1972 by Taranaki Newspapers Ltd., is also important. (For a time Griffin was Teira's doctor in Ōpunake.) On 20 November 1909 the *Star* published 'Hori Teira's "Aitua": The Story of a Retribution', in which James Cowan recounts a conversation he had with Teira in a Wellington hotel. That

account was widely republished in other newspapers, including in the *Auckland Star* on 6 August 1935, the year Teira died. The 26 March 1910 edition of the *Taranaki Herald* has Teira's own account of events both before and after Wairau. Cowan's 1955 publication, *The New Zealand Wars: A History of the Maori Campaigns and the Pioneering Period: Volume I: 1845–1864* (Wellington: R. E. Owen), also includes references to Teira, as does Dick Scott's *Ask That Mountain: The Story of Parihaka* (Auckland: Heinemann & Southern Cross, 1975).

44 The rohe of Ngāti Ruanui is in South Taranaki.

45 From the article 'Days of Strife', *New Zealand Herald*, 7 May 1934.

46 Griffin, *Tales of Te Namu and Hori Teira*, 27.

47 *Hawke's Bay Herald*, 8 July 1863. The *Herald* also reported that on 20 June that year the board listing the various tolls levied on people and goods passing through the gate was seized by solders of the 57th Regiment and taken to New Plymouth, and thence to Auckland, on board the *Eclipse*.

48 Griffin, *Tales of Te Namu and Hori Teira*, 15.

49 These details are from Rex Wright-St Clair's prodigious *Historia Nunc Vivat: Medical Practitioners in New Zealand, 1840 to 1930* (Christchurch: Cotter Medical History Trust, 2003), which contains information on some 3000 people who served in the medical profession in Aotearoa between 1840 and 1930. There is an interesting aspect of the entry on Dr Hope: according to Wright-St Clair (who was the son of a Māori Land Court interpreter), 'Hope had attended [Teira] previously, [and had] argued and threatened him with his sword.' The cause of the argument is not recorded, but Griffin has Hope holding a bayonet (not a sword) to Teira's throat, which 'then marked him [Hope] as Teira's man in the Ambush' (*Tales of Te Namu and Hori Teira*, 24).

50 On 2 June the *Southland Times* carried a lengthy account of events from the only member of the 57th to survive the ambush, Private Florence Kelly.

51 *Daily Southern Cross*, 4 July 1863.

52 *Taranaki Daily News*, 26 March 1910.

53 James Cowan, *The New Zealand Wars: A History of the Maori*

Campaigns and the Pioneer Period (Wellington: Skinner/Government Printer, 1922), 218.

54 I don't think that this is the land sold to Kate Gilhooly in 1921. Hori Teira did not gain title to Parihaka A until 1916, but Dick Scott has him on the Pungarehu land in 1897.

55 The quote is taken from the preface to Cowan, *The New Zealand Wars.*

56 David Hastings, *The Many Deaths of Mary Dobie: Murder, Politics and Revenge in Nineteenth-Century New Zealand* (Auckland: Auckland University Press, 2015), 126.

57 Griffin, *Tales of Te Namu and Hori Teira.* On his death in 1935 the Pākehā press may have described Hori Teira as a settler, but the Ōpunake Register refers to him as a 'Maori of full blood' (p. 46).

58 Keenan (*Te Whiti o Rongomai*) explains that Te Whiti o Rongomai's baptismal name was Eruera, although he was often referred to as Erueti, including by the German Lutheran missionary Johann Riemenschneider, with whom Te Whiti lived and studied for a time at Riemenschneider's mission station in Wārea.

59 *Taranaki Minute Book No. 4*, pp. 70–71.

60 Wai 143, p. 238.

61 Wai 143 I17(g), p. 46.

62 The comment, which is unattributed, appears in *The First 100 Years: Catholic Faith on the Taranaki Coast*, a booklet prepared by Ian Patrick Stephenson for the 1999 centennial celebration of the establishment of the Ōpunake parish (Ōpunake: Our Lady Star of the Sea Parish, 1999).

63 This is from the report published in the *Hawera & Normanby Star*. Newton King had previously been one of three shareholders in the Crown Dairy company, which in 1897 sold its plant to the newly formed Cape Egmont Co-op Dairy Co. Prior to the First World War his stock and station agency was reputedly the largest privately owned company in the southern hemisphere.

64 *AJHR* 1894, H-23, p. 13.

65 Buchanan, *Ko Taranaki Te Maunga.*

66 Espiner's observation was made in a presentation to *Waitohu: Women Reclaiming The Ink*, a celebration of mana wāhine hosted by the

National Library Te Puna Mātauranga o Aotearoa in October 2020. The reference to traumascapes is from Maria Tumarkin, *Traumascapes: The Power and Fate of Places Transformed by Tragedy* (Melbourne: Melbourne University Press, 2005).

67 Wai 143 I17, p. 7.

68 Ibid., p. 242.

69 Buchanan, *The Parihaka Album*, 53. Buchanan also refers to a footnote in Scott's *Ask That Mountain*, which mentions that the 1890 *Taranaki Holiday Guide* listed Parihaka as a tourist destination, warning against getting lost among its lanes and alleys.

Kate

1 The executors and trustees of Andrew's estate were James Barry of Hastings and Andrew's brother-in-law Richard Fleming (Kate's older half-brother). In a codicil signed in 1922 Barry is replaced by Andrew's son, Andy. In that codicil is written: 'Andrew Gilhooly his mark', next to which is a small, ragged cross. The lawyer points out that my great-grandfather is 'literate and in full function of his mental faculties but unable to write his name owing to his hand and arm being affected by paralysis agitans'. A year later that disease would appear on his death certificate.

2 When Kate died, her will specified that her sons Hugh and Andy were to be trustees of an estate valued at £10,800 (around $648,000 in today's terms). Her daughters, Liz and Moll, were given equal shares in her house in New Plymouth, its furniture and Kate's personal effects. Her third son, Tom, was offered first option of purchasing her farm at Pungarehu — 'ninety eight acres one rood one perch more or less' — from her estate.

Vocation

1 The details in this paragraph are from searches of the Papers Past website, https://paperspast.natlib.govt.nz/.

2 Taranaki Rugby Union, *One Hundred Years of Taranaki Rugby, 1885–1985* (New Plymouth: TNL Ltd, 1985), 37.

3 William K. Howitt, *A Pioneer Looks Back Again* (Auckland: Oswald-Sealy, 1947), 70.

4 *Opunake Times*, 24 July 1919. Hugh would later chair the Hall Committee for twenty-one years.

5 The details of Dick's years at Sacred Heart are from digitised versions of the school yearbooks.

6 I received photocopies of the letters from Mary Kelly, librarian at the Holy Cross Seminary's archives, in February 2019. Mary also sent me a digital copy of a photo of Dick taken in 1929 with classmates at Saddle Hill, a copy of an entry in the *New Zealand Tablet* (dated 20 July 1932), which mentions his attaining his doctorate of divinity, and a digital copy of Dick's ordination card.

7 Borgia to O'Shea, 19 October 1924, CAWA.

8 O'Shea to Borgia, 22 October 1924, HCSA.

9 Gilhooly to Morkane, 28 November 1924, HCSA.

10 At the time the Pungarehu parish was part of the archdiocese of Wellington, but in 1980 it became part of the new diocese of Palmerston North.

11 Gilhooly to Morkane, 27 December 1924, HCSA.

12 Gilhooly to Morkane, 28 December 1925, HCSA.

13 The letter is part of Hagan's papers (HAG/1/1930, p. 2305). The *Tablet* was a Catholic periodical published weekly in Dunedin between 1873 and 1996.

14 Heather McNamara, '*The New Zealand Tablet* and the Irish Catholic Press Worldwide, 1898–1923', *New Zealand Journal of History* 37, no. 2 (2003): 157.

15 Hagan's contribution to the establishment of an independent Irish state is covered in Dermott Keogh's 'John Hagan and Radical Irish Nationalism: 1916–1930: A Study in Political Catholicism', in *The Irish College, Rome, and Its World*, eds Daire Keogh and Albert McDonnell (Dublin: Four Courts Press, 2008), 242–57. Kelly's career is described in Rory Sweetman's chapter in the same publication, '"Waving the Green Flag" in the Southern Hemisphere: The Kellys and the Irish College, Rome'.

16 Nicolas Reid, *Churchman: A Study of James Michael Liston, Bishop of Auckland 1920–70* (PhD thesis, University of Auckland, 2004), 89, 199.

Are we there yet?

1 McRae to Morkane, 12 March 1930, CAWA.

2 Both Archbishop O'Shea and Father McRae lived at Paterson Street, the former between 1909 and 1950. Dick was also there between 1935 and 1940, so he was well known to both the chancellor and the archbishop.

3 The photo of McRae can be accessed at https://natlib.govt.nz/records/22594578. The baptismal anecdote is recounted by Peter Holm, the archivist at CAWA. I visited Peter with Camille on 16 March 2019, and then again in September 2020. On the first trip Peter put folder CAWA 439 f.2 in front of us. It contained thirty-one discrete items: twelve letters from Dick (all of them to Father McRae), thirteen additional pieces of correspondence either to Dick or about him, and six other artefacts (copies of two wills, two money orders, his exam results in 1931, and a 1932 telegram from Dick to Archbishop O'Shea which reads simply: 'Returning home health reasons — Gilhooly').

4 The quote is from Michael Smith, 'Life at the Irish College during the Second Vatican Council', in *The Irish College, Rome, and Its World*, eds Daire Keogh and Albert McDonnell (Dublin: Four Courts Press, 2008), 258.

5 Andrew's will provided for the 'suitable maintenance and education' of the Gilhooly children until they turned twenty-one, so Dick still met that requirement.

6 Curran served as rector of the college from 1930 to 1939, having taken over from the long-standing John Hagan (1904–30).

7 Students from the Irish College had historically studied at Propaganda College, but by the early twentieth century they were increasingly enrolling at the Lateran.

Via dei Ss Quattro

1 Rory Sweetman, '"Waving the Green Flag" in the Southern Hemisphere: The Kellys and the Irish College, Rome', in *The Irish College, Rome, and Its World*, eds Diare Keogh and Albert McDonnell (Dublin: Four Courts Press, 2008), 205.

2 Keogh ('John Hagan and Radical Irish Nationalism: 1916–1930: A Study in Political Catholicism', in *The Irish College, Rome, and Its*

World, 245) describes the college 'as an important centre for Irish nationalist "diplomats" during the 1920s' and assesses the significance of Rector Hagan's lengthy correspondences with both Séan T. O'Kelly, future president of Ireland, and Éamon de Valera. De Valera visited the college more than once, during one of which meetings, in 1926, Hagan appears to have provided the theological legitimation for the establishment of de Valera's new party, Fianna Fáil.

3 Colin Barr, 'The Irish College, Rome, and the Appointment of Irish Bishops to the United States, 1830–1851', in *The Irish College, Rome, and Its World*, 102–15.

4 Patrick Corish, 'The Beginnings of the Irish College, Rome', in *The Irish College, Rome, and Its World*, 1–13. Three hundred years later the Irish still enjoyed a reputation for being 'difficult to handle' (Sweetman, '"Waving the Green Flag"', 210).

5 Fearghus Ó Fearghail tells the full tale in his chapter 'Daniel O'Connell's Roman Bequest', in *The Irish College, Rome, and Its World*, 83–101.

6 Gilhooly to McRae, 20 November 1930, CAWA.

7 McRae to Gilhooly, 21 February 1931, CAWA. Each of McRae's letters to Dick is typed, whereas all of the other correspondence I have found about or from Dick is handwritten.

8 Gilhooly to McRae, 19 April 1931, CAWA. At the bottom of the last page of the letter appears the Latin phrase *Ora Pro Me* ('pray for me'). It is not in Dick's hand (nor McRae's) and has clearly been appended, perhaps after Paterson Street had received news of Dick's illness in late 1932 or even later, following his death in 1955.

9 Gilhooly to McRae, 6 June 1931, CAWA.

10 The quote is from page 371 of Douglas Copland, 'New Zealand's Economic Difficulties and Expert Opinion', *The Economic Journal* 42, no. 167 (1932): 371–79.

11 This detail is taken from the formal record of Dick's examination results held in the CAWA. There are some fascinating courses that he did not take, including *Archaeologiae Sacrae*, *Metaphysicae Superioris* and *Ethicae*.

12 Gilhooly to McRae, 7 November 1931, CAWA.

13 The 31st International Eucharistic Congress took place in Dublin during 22–26 June 1932, when Dick was at the sharp end of his DD. While 25 per cent of the entire population of the Republic of Ireland was busy attending the final Mass of the Congress, Dick was immersing himself in doctrinal minutiae.

14 Curran to O'Shea, 3 December 1931, CAWA.

Zenith

1 McRea to Gilhooly, 9 January 1932, CAWA.

2 O'Shea to Curran, 23 January 1932, CAWA.

3 Curran to O'Shea, 4 March 1932, CAWA.

4 Gilhooly to McRae, 13 March 1932, CAWA.

5 Nicolas Reid, *Churchman: A Study of James Michael Liston, Bishop of Auckland 1920–70* (PhD thesis, University of Auckland, 2004), 42.

6 McRea to Gilhooly, 3 May 1932, CAWA.

7 O'Shea to Curran, 16 May 1932, CAWA.

8 Gilhooly to McRae, 22 July 1932, CAWA.

9 The obituary is undated and unattributed, and I came across it lying in a photo album that once belonged to Dick's younger sister Liz.

10 *New Zealand Tablet*, 20 July 1932.

11 Emily Dickinson [1914], *The Single Hound: Poems of a Lifetime* (Surrey, UK: Alma Classics, 2018), 5.

12 Vincent O'Sullivan, 'The Club', in *Selected Stories* (Wellington: Victoria University Press, 2019), 186.

13 Helen Small, *The Value of the Humanities* (Oxford: Oxford University Press, 2013), 74.

Nadir

1 Sabbatucci is long gone, of course, but the building in which he had his rooms is still there. I wandered past it during our trip to Rome in autumn 2019. There are no doctors now — it's all travel agents and insurance salespeople.

2 My deep thanks go to Martina Depentor, formerly of the Commercial and Cultural Promotion section of the Italian Embassy in Wellington, for her generous (and rapid) translation of Sabbatucci's words.

3 Kyne to O'Shea, 6 August 1932, CAWA. He also enclosed a copy of Sabbatucci's letter (in the original Italian), which is how it made its way from Rome to Wellington. John Anthony 'Jack' Kyne, an Irishman, had also studied for the priesthood at the Irish College and, like Dick, was also ordained at the age of twenty-two. He was appointed vice-rector of the college in 1930.

4 Rory Sweetman, '"Waving the Green Flag" in the Southern Hemisphere: The Kellys and the Irish College, Rome', in *The Irish College, Rome, and Its World*, eds Daire Keogh and Albert McDonnell (Dublin: Four Courts Press, 2008), 209, 214.

Homecoming

1 Gilhooly to McRae, 18 August 1932, CAWA.

2 Gilhooly to McRae, 5 May 1933, CAWA.

3 Gilhooly to O'Shea, 16 May 1933, CAWA.

4 Gilhooly to O'Shea, 16 November 1933, CAWA.

Silence

1 Dick's character reference is from the April 1935 edition of the *Catholic News*. An earlier edition ran an article called 'Who Is Your Patron Saint?', in which I learnt the patron saints for actors (St Genesius), comedians (St Vitus), those who are 'deaf and dumb' (St John of Beverly), domestics (St Zita), pawnbrokers (St Nicholas of Myra), tax-gatherers and civil servants (St Matthew) and university students (who for some reason get three, the first two of whom are heavyweights: St Thomas, St Paul and St Albert).

2 Neil Vaney's MA thesis *The Dual Tradition: Irish Catholics and French Priests in New Zealand — the West Coast Experience, 1865–1910* (Canterbury University, 1976) also explores anti-Catholic sentiment during the First World War, triggered in part by (then Bishop) O'Shea's attempts to prevent ecclesiastical students and Marist priests from being conscripted.

3 Two years earlier, following a request from Archbishop O'Shea, Fraser had prevented a series of anti-Catholic public lectures from taking place at the Paramount Theatre in Wellington. Fraser's views may

have been shaped by the informal alliance that developed between the newly formed Labour Party and the Catholic Church during the First World War. At that time the *New Zealand Tablet*, under James Kelly's editorship, had opposed the conscription of religious and conscientious objectors (Fraser spent a year in prison for his stance against conscription), and had not taken an uncritically pro-Allied editorial line (teara.govt.nz/en/biographies/3k6/kelly-james-joseph/print).

4 McRae to Gilhooly, 17 April 1951, PNDA.

5 Gilhooly to McRae, 25 November 1951, PNDA.

6 Gilhooly to McRae, 10 June 1951, PNDA.

7 Gilhooly to McRae, 8 July 1951, PNDA.

8 Gilhooly to McRae, 2 September 1951, PNDA.

9 Gilhooly to McRae, 12 December 1951, PNDA.

10 Gilhooly to McRae, 10 June 1951, PNDA.

Bob/TB redux

1 There is another, more tenuous connection. Dad's regiment was formed in 1948 by the amalgamation of the Wellington West Coast and Taranaki regiments. The history of the latter ran all the way back through the 11th (Taranaki Rifles) Regiment to the Taranaki Rifle Volunteers — who, of course, were present at Parihaka.

2 The Home was opened on 29 October 1921 and closed its doors to orphans in 1978, reopening in 1987 as the Homeleigh Christian School. In the Masterton District: Registered Heritage Items the Home is described as 'a handsome large villa in an English Cottage style, fashionable at the time, though there are references to Dutch gables in the third floor roof and roof treatment. The building is . . . of some historic and architectural value.'

3 From Mike Chunn, *A Sharp Left Turn: Notes on a Life in Music, from Split Enz to Play it Strange* (Auckland: Allen & Unwin, 2019), 109.

4 Henderson's views are contained in the formal assessment of Dad's teaching performance that was submitted to the Department of Education following his first inspection visit on 17 June 1965.

5 Obituaries, *Manawatu Herald*, 23 June 1927, p. 2.

Death

1 From Cormack McCarthy, *Suttree* (New York: Random House, 1978).

2 From Tim Winton, *Cloudstreet* (Carlton, VIC: McPhee Gribble, 1991).

Conversations with the dead

1 Paul Auster, *4 3 2 1* (London: Faber and Faber, 2017), 364.

2 Ibid.

3 Vivian Gornick, *The Odd Woman and the City* (Carlton, VIC: Nero, 2015).

4 Benjamin Iveson, John Conly and John B. Dawson, *The First Hundred Years: Centennial Survey of Masterton Methodism 1858–1958* (Masterton: Masterton Central and Solway Methodist Church Trustees, 1958), 8.

5 Gilhooly to O'Shea, 5 May 1933, CAWA.

6 Neil Vaney, *The Dual Tradition: Irish Catholics and French Priests in New Zealand — the West Coast Experience, 1865–1910* (MA thesis, Canterbury University, 1976).

7 Mary Goulter tells Cognet's story in *Sons of France: A Forgotten Influence in New Zealand History* (Wellington: Whitcomb & Tombs, 1957).

8 Vaney, *The Dual Tradition.*

9 Patrick Joseph Power, *The Church in Taranaki (New Zealand): A Sketch Prepared for the Jubilee of the Hawera Parish, 1875–1925* (Dunedin: *New Zealand Tablet*, 1925), 24.

10 In 1927 O'Shea closed the Māori Mission in Ōkato and folded the parish into the Ōpunake parish. The decision to remove the last of the French Marists at Ōkato, Father Menard, did not go down well with Pākehā parishioners. In a petition to O'Shea they expressed concern that Menard's departure would mean that the local Māori, 'simple souls for the most part', would 'drift back to the easy life of the pah' (from a 1927 petition addressed to 'The Right Reverend Archbishop O'Shea' from 'Your Grace's Parishioners of the Parish of Okato', PNDA).

11 Father Michael Doolaghty buried my great-grandfather in the Ōkato cemetery in 1923. Some fourteen years later, as Chris van der Krogt explains in his PhD thesis *More a Part than Apart: The Catholic*

Community in New Zealand Society, 1918 to 1940 (Massey University, 1994), Doolaghty was the parish priest in Taihape, where he asked Archbishop O'Shea's permission for a 'mixed' marriage — one of a Catholic to a non-Catholic — to be celebrated before the altar. At the time such marriages were frowned on by the Church and permission was duly denied. They were still frowned on when my parents were planning to marry twenty years later, which goes a long way to explaining my father's conversion to Catholicism.

Reckoning

1 Hilary Mantel, *The Mirror and the Light* (London: 4th Estate, 2020), 615.

2 Wai 143, pp. 91–92. Peter Adds calculates that 1,275,000 acres were confiscated (Peter Adds, 'Te Muru me te Raupatu: The Aftermath', in *Contested Ground: Te Whenua I Tohea: The Taranaki Wars 1860–1881*, ed. Kelvin Day (Wellington: Huia, 2010), 255–61.

3 Wai 143, p. 193.

4 Avirl Bell, 'Reverberating Historical Privilege of a "Middling" Sort of Settler Family', *Genealogy* 4, no. 46 (2020), doi:10.3390/genealogy4020046.

5 Wai 143, pp. 309–10.

6 Ibid., p. 133.

7 Patrick Joseph Power, *The Church in Taranaki (New Zealand): A Sketch Prepared for the Jubilee of the Hawera Parish, 1875–1925* (Dunedin: *New Zealand Tablet*, 1925), 14.

8 Richard Hill, 'War and Police: The Armed Constabulary in the Taranaki Wars', in *Contested Ground*, 205–30.

9 Ruth Edwards, *An Atlas of Irish History*, 3rd ed. (London: Routledge, 2005), 161.

10 See, for example, ibid., 163.

11 Wai 143, p. 113.

12 Robert Macfarlane, *The Old Ways: A Journey on Foot* (London: Penguin, 2013), 13.

13 Wai 143, p. 127. The reference was to the New Zealand Settlement Act 1863 and its subsequent amendments.

14 Alan Ward, 'Law and Law-enforcement on the New Zealand Frontier, 1840–1893', *New Zealand Journal of History* 5, no. 2 (2003): 145–46. Ward concludes that 'the concept of "the rule of law" was prostituted and degraded in the pursuit of white supremacy and the acquisition of Maori land' (p. 148).

15 Mantel, *The Mirror and the Light*, 846.

16 The legislation was passed in August. A month later, the Amnesty Act authorised the governor to grant amnesty to Māori who had been 'in insurrection against Her Majesty's authority' on the west coast of the North Island. Much later, in 1981 the head of the New Zealand Police Force apologised for the AC's role in the invasion of Parihaka (Rachel Buchanan, 'Beating Shame: Parihaka and the Very Long Sorry', *Te Pouhere Kōrero* 6 [2012]).

17 Wai 143, p. 204. Bryce may have been parroting the West Coast Commission's recipe for peace 'at the doors of Parihaka, [where] the establishment of English homesteads and the fencing and cultivation of the lands, will be a guarantee of peace' (Buchanan, *The Parihaka Album: Lest We Forget* [Wellington: Huia, 2009], 44).

18 Wai 143, p. 134.

19 Te Ture Haeata ki Parihaka/Parihaka Reconciliation Act 2019, p. 16.

Telling stories

1 Vivian Gornick, *The Odd Woman and the City* (Carlton, VIC: Nero, 2015).

2 Rachel Buchanan, *The Parihaka Album: Lest We Forget* (Wellington: Huia, 2009), 75.

3 Ibid.

4 Hugh Campbell explores the making of the colonial farm in Aotearoa in his superb *Farming Inside Invisible Worlds: Modernist Agriculture and its Consequences* (London: Bloomsbury Academic, 2020).

5 Ibid., 45.

6 Moana Jackson, 'Where to next? Decolonisation and the Stories in the Land', *The Spinoff*, 7 March 2020.

7 Campbell, *Farming Inside Invisible Worlds*.

8 Kelvin Day, *Contested Ground: Te Whenua I Tohea: The Taranaki Wars 1860–1881* (Wellington: Huia, 2010), xix.
9 One of the best guides through these issues is Danny Keenan's *Wars Without End. Ngā Pakanga Whenua O Mua: New Zealand's Land Wars — A Māori Perspective*, 2nd ed. (Auckland: Penguin Random House, 2021).

Beneficiary of injustice

1 On page 40 of Dinah Hawken's long-form poem *There Is No Harbour* (Wellington: Victoria University Press, 2019) sits the line: 'I am the beneficiary of injustice.' As a clean, powerful statement of my inheritance, that is much better than anything I can come up with as a title to this chapter.
2 In this section I have used the Reserve Bank of New Zealand's online calculator, which draws on historical quarterly consumer price index (CPI) data to estimate equivalent contemporary prices. My calculations need to be taken with a fair bit of salt, partly as land is not one of the categories from which CPI rates are built, and because I'm comparing across both time and space as far as the relative values of leases are concerned.
3 Christine Sleeter, 'Inheriting Footholds and Cushions: Family Legacies and Institutional Racism', in *Crafting Critical Stories: Toward Pedagogies and Methodologies of Collaboration, Inclusion, and Voice*, eds Judith Flores-Carmona and Kristin Luschen (New York: Peter Lang, 2014), 11–26.
4 Belinda Borell, Helen Moewaka Barnes and Tim McCreanor, 'Conceptualising Historical Privilege: The Flip Side of Historical Trauma, a Brief Examination', *AlterNative* 14, no. 1 (2017): 25–34.

The hardest word

1 Rachel Buchanan, *Ko Taranaki Te Maunga* (Wellington: Bridget Williams Books, 2018), 71.

Ending the forgetting

1 Rachel Buchanan, *The Parihaka Album: Lest We Forget* (Wellington: Huia, 2009), 71.

2 Avril Bell, 'Decolonizing Conviviality and "Becoming Ordinary": Crosscultural Face-to-face Encounters in Aotearoa New Zealand', *Ethnic and Racial Studies* 39, no. 7 (2016): 1170–86.

3 Ibid., 1174.

4 John Newton, 'Becoming Pākehā', *Landfall* 218 (2009): 38–48.

5 Avril Bell, 'Recognition or Ethics?', *Cultural Studies* 22, no. 6 (2008): 850–69.

6 Bell, 'Decolonizing Conviviality', 1175.

7 Robert Macfarlane, *The Old Ways: A Journey on Foot* (London: Penguin, 2013), xi.

8 Avril Bell explains Ghassan Hage's idea of movable roots in her article 'Moving Roots: A "Small Story" of Settler History and Home Places', *Qualitative Inquiry* 23, no. 6 (2017): 452–57.

9 Paula Savage, 'Parihaka: The Weighty Legacy of Unfinished Business', in *Parihaka: The Art of Passive Resistance*, eds Te Miringa Hohaia, Gregory O'Brien and Lara Strongman (Wellington: Victoria University Press, 2005), 14.

10 Alison Jones, 'The Limits of Cross-cultural Dialogue: Pedagogy, Desire and Absolution in the Classroom', *Educational Theory* 49, no. 3 (1999): 299–316.

11 Ursula K. Le Guin, 'Introduction to Rocannon's World', in *Ursula K. Le Guin: Hainish Novels & Stories*, Vol. 1, ed. Brian Attebery (New York: Library of America, 2017), 761.

Acknowledgements

1 Rachel Buchanan and Maria Tumarkin, 'Bread and Breadth: Two Reflections on the Ethics of (Doing) History', *Australian Humanities Review* 52 (2012): 82.

Acknowledgements

I would like to thank, first of all, the archivists — 'the "secret historians" . . . the first authors of the histories we make' — who helped me find Andrew and Dick.[1] The pieces were all there (whether hiding or waiting I cannot say), but they were strewn about in various places I had little or no familiarity with. I needed guides and found some excellent ones.

Alice and Caroline, research archivists at Archives New Zealand Te Rua Mahara o te Kāwanatanga in Wellington and Christchurch respectively, have been exceptionally helpful, locating Andrew's service record and the documents associated with the purchase of Section 44 of the Cape Survey District.

Patrick, from LINZ, patiently (and over quite a few emails) walked me through the process of obtaining historic titles to the three farms.

Anne Eddy and her colleagues at the Taranaki Research Centre Te Pua Wānanga o Taranaki at Puke Ariki in New Plymouth made time and space for me to look through their records for signs of Andrew, and Mike Gooch sent me copies of the cadastral maps mentioned here.

Peter Holm, who works at the Catholic Archdiocese of Wellington Archives, arranged for Camille and me to have access to the material the Church holds on Dick. Sophia Macris at the Palmerston North diocesan office led me to Dick's 1951 exchange of letters with McRae.

Kerry Plamus from the Sacred Heart Old Boys' Association put me onto its fantastic digitised database of yearbooks, and Mary Kelly, librarian at the archives of the Holy Cross Seminary, mailed me copies of the first of Dick's letters.

Alice, Caroline, Patrick, Anne, Mike, Peter, Sophia, Kerry and Mary: thank you for bringing Andrew and Dick back into the light.

Cezara Auluzena Petrina, the archivist at the Pontifical Irish College, introduced me to Ricardus, Andreas and Catarina Gilhooly — my thanks are due to her and to Rector Ciaran O'Carroll for having so warmly welcomed Ema, Camille and me into the building in which my great-uncle studied and lived nearly a century ago. Thanks too, and apologies, to the determined librarian from the Lateran University whose name I have forgotten and who tried valiantly to track the damn thesis down.

The only reason I know that Hori Teira sold Parihaka A to Kate Gilhooly is because Tinei Tautiaga Mamea from the Waitangi Tribunal Te Rōpū Whakamana i te Tiriti o Waitangi generously retrieved and sent me the entire record that informs Wai 143 I17. Tēnā koe, Tinei.

I last saw Rachel Buchanan some forty years ago on the stage of the State Insurance Building in New Plymouth. *The Wizard of Oz*, in which she sang the lead role, is a disturbing show in which things are out of kilter and not quite right. Buchanan's piercing, humane writing on Parihaka exposes the events of November 1881, as well as their consequences, in ways which compelled me to confront my own connection to that place of power. Thank you, Rachel.

Ria Waikerepuru, of Taranaki Whānui, Ngāpuhi and Te Arawa, is Kaiwhakarato Pārongo Rangahau Māori at Massey University. Ria: heartfelt thanks and deep gratitude for your wise advice and guidance. Avril Bell, Therese Crocker, Helen Dollery, Janine Hayward, Ella Kahu, Bernard Leuthart, Mike Spedding and Hazel Tidman are precious friends and outstanding people. Each read earlier drafts of this book and it is the better for their gentle words of correction and encouragement.

Thanks, too, to my cousins Judi Altinkaya, Di Tracey and Cathy Tracey, who offered constructive and nuanced comments on a paper I gave at a conference a while ago that was based on parts of this book. There is an art form to telling someone that perhaps there is a better way of conveying certain ideas. The art is not that widely practised, but they are good at it.

I owe a debt to Nicola Legat at Massey University Press, who saw something worth pursuing in the rag-tag of notes I put before her a couple of years ago. And to Anna Bowbyes and Matt Turner (and, in fact, to everyone at MUP, who make beautiful books): thank you for 'thingifying' those notes so wonderfully!

Finally, I wish to thank the three women who made me a father. Camille guided me calmly and expertly around the world of archives, and was with me when I first encountered Dick through his correspondence. Rosalie is a sociologist by nature, one of the sharpest people I know and an outstanding cook to boot: towards the end of the project, in particular, I did not want for sustenance. And Ema stopped my brain from imploding on 14 January 2019, and was my first and most important reader. *Toujours, ma belle.*

MASSEY
UNIVERSITY
PRESS

First published in 2021 by Massey University Press
Private Bag 102904, North Shore Mail Centre
Auckland 0745, New Zealand
www.masseypress.ac.nz

Design by Kate Barraclough
Cover photograph copyright © Richard Shaw
Endpapers: New Zealand Land and Survey maps of Wairau
and Cape, 1885 (front), and West Coast, 1880 (back),
courtesy Puke Ariki

A catalogue record for this book is available from the
National Library of New Zealand

Printed and bound in China by Everbest Investment Ltd

ISBN: 978-0-9951431-4-2
eISBN: 978-0-9951465-2-5

Tapuae
Timaru
Katikara
Kaihihi
Hangatahua (Stony River)
Werekino
SOUTH ROAD
OAKURA BLOCK
HAURANGA
KORU
HURFORD RD
BARRETT RD
CARRINGTON RD
MANGORFI RD
KENT RD
PITONE RD
LEITH RD
PERTH RD
HAMPDEN RD
Okato
OKATO
Block
POUAKAI RANGE
8700 . 0 . 0
6000 . 0 . 0 (Open)
PUNEHU
STONY RIVER
7000 . 0 . 0 (Forest)
Total 18000
13.000 . 0 . 0
2000 . 0 . 0
3000 . 0 . 0
BELLS FALLS
IKAROA
15000 . 0 . 0 (Open)
PARIHAKA
Mount Egmont 8270 FT
25000 . 0 . 0
9000 . 0 . 0
7000 . 0 . 0
TIPOKA
Total 56.000
PARIHAKA
NGARIKI
6000 . 0 . 0
PROVINCIAL FOREST RES
9000 . 0 . 0
4000.0.0
16.000 . 0
Moutoti
Oao-iti
SIX MILES RADIUS
21.000 . 0 . 0 (Forest)
Total 44000
OPUNAKE
Hursthouse's Line
3000 . 0 . 0
Waiwiri
NUKUTE APIAPI
8000 . 0 . 0 (Open)
UMUROA
NINE MILES RADIUS
Okawea
Total 26000
Total 14
OPUNAKE
Otahi
13.000 . 0 . 0 (Forest)
OEO
Waiaua
Mangahume
Waiteika
Taungatara
6000 . 0 . 0 (Open)
Punehu
OMUTURANGI
TE AUROA
TAIKATU
OEO
Puketapu
Ouri

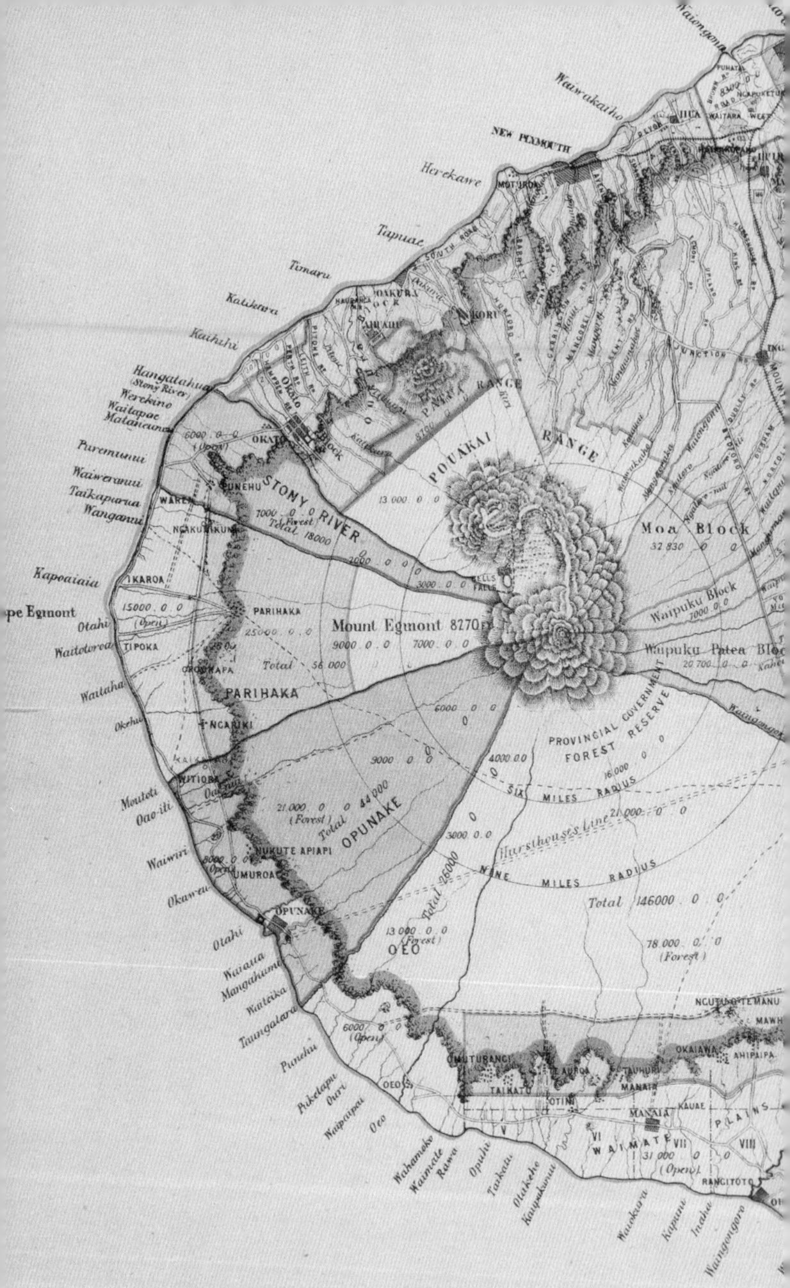

NEW PLYMOUTH
Waiwakaiho
Waiongona
Herekawe
MOTUROA
Tapuae
Timaru
Kaitetara
Kaihihi
OAKURA
BLOCK
SOUTH ROAD
Hangatahua (Stony River)
Werekino
Waitapae
Matanaunui
Puremunui
Waiweranui
Taikapirua
Wanganui
Okato
OKATO
Block
PAHAKA RANGE
POUAKAI RANGE
STONY RIVER
PUNEHU
WAREA
NGAKUMIKUMI
Kapoaiaia
IKAROA
Cape Egmont
Otahi
Waitotorea
TIPOKA
PARIHAKA
Mount Egmont 8270 Ft
13.000. 0. 0
7000. 0. 0
3000. 0. 0
15000. 0. 0
(Open)
25000. 0. 0
9000. 0. 0
Total 56.000
Waitaha
OROUKAPA
PARIHAKA
Okehu
NGARIKI
KAIKAURA
NITIORA
Moutoti
Oao-iti
Waiwiri
NUKUTE APIAPI
UMUROA
Okawa
OPUNAKE
Otahi
Waiaua
Mangahume
Waiteika
Taungatara
Punehu
Puketapu
Ouri
Waipaipai
Oeo
OEO
21.000. 0. 0
(Forest)
Total 44.000
OPUNAKE
Total 26000
13.000. 0. 0
(Forest)
6000. 0. 0
(Open)
Moa Block
32.830. 0. 0
Waipuku Block
7000. 0. 0
Waipuku Patea Block
20.700. 0. 0
PROVINCIAL GOVERNMENT FOREST RESERVE
16.000. 0. 0
4000.0.0
SIX MILES RADIUS
Hursthouse's Line
21.000. 0. 0
NINE MILES RADIUS
Total 146000. 0. 0
78.000. 0. 0
(Forest)
NGUTUOTEMANU
OKAIAWA
AHIPAIPA
OMUTURANGI
TAIKATU
OTINI
MANAIA
KAUAE
PLAINS
WAIMATE
31.000. 0. 0
(Open)
RANGITOTO
Wahamoko
Waimate
Rawa
Opuhi
Taikatu
Otakeho
Kaupokonui
Waiokura
Kapuni
Inaha
Waingongoro
JUNCTION ROAD